LEARNING TO SUCCEED

LEARNING TO SUCCEED

Rethinking Corporate Education in a World of Unrelenting Change

Jason Wingard

AMACOM

American Management Association
New York • Atlanta • Brussels • Chicago • Mexico City
San Francisco • Shanghai • Tokyo • Toronto • Washington, D.C.

This publication is designed to provide accurate and authoritative information in regard to the subject matter covered. It is sold with the understanding that the publisher is not engaged in rendering legal, accounting, or other professional service. If legal advice or other expert assistance is required, the services of a competent professional person should be sought.

Library of Congress Cataloging-in-Publication Data

Wingard, Jason.
   Learning to succeed : rethinking corporate education in a world of unrelenting change / Jason Wingard.
      pages cm
   Includes bibliographical references and index.
   ISBN 978-0-8144-3413-0 (hardcover) — ISBN 978-0-8144-3414-7 (ebook)
1. Organizational learning. 2. Employees—Training of. I. Title.
   HD58.82.W557 2015
   658.3'124—dc23   2014042808

About AMA
American Management Association (www.amanet.org) is a world leader in talent development, advancing the skills of individuals to drive business success. Our mission is to support the goals of individuals and organizations through a complete range of products and services, including classroom and virtual seminars, webcasts, webinars, podcasts, conferences, corporate and government solutions, business books, and research. AMA's approach to improving performance combines experiential learning—learning through doing—with opportunities for ongoing professional growth at every step of one's career journey.

Printing number
10 9 8 7 6 5 4 3 2 1

For my grandmother, Alice Potts Wingard,
in memoriam.

CONTENTS

FOREWORD

I have always believed that people are a company's greatest asset and, in today's environment, where the competition for top talent is more intense than ever before, developing and retaining the best and brightest is a nonnegotiable for success. At a time when the world is rapidly transforming and growing more complex, companies need to continuously train their people in the new skills they will need for success. At the same time, growth and development opportunities have become increasingly critical criteria in the career choices of the best talent, and an investment in them, through training and educational programs, is an investment in the long-term future of a company. Simply put, learning and development is a core competency that any company absolutely has to master in order to win in today's marketplace.

At PepsiCo, we have established a comprehensive learning organization that values and prioritizes professional development for every employee throughout the company. Executives and managers are regularly trained in core leadership skills, as well as in specific functional best practices. Leveraging a wide variety of training methods, our Talent Management Development and Training team partners work with our business units to create innovative learning experiences customized for our people's needs and corporate challenges. Most important, our learning initiatives link directly to our company's strategic goals. Targeted programs aligned with our business objectives achieve the best results and contribute to our company's performance. Our leadership team is committed to excellence in everything we do at PepsiCo, and our suite of learning and development opportunities is one of the fundamental tools we use to achieve this goal.

Learning to Succeed highlights the changing competitive landscape in business and the risk corporations face if they do not adapt to, and prepare for it. The interlocking connection between corporate strategy and learning creates the necessary formula not just to remain relevant, but to thrive in the new global context. The book astutely maps that formula's dependence on foundational elements, such as C-suite sponsorship, structural innovation, and a cultural aptitude for change, while also pinpointing the roadblocks that organizations will need to overcome to become fully functioning learning organizations. In the end, *Learning to Succeed* is a guide for business advantage through corporate learning and development, and it demonstrates how to maximize continuous returns on investment.

Jason Wingard is a leading authority in the field of corporate education. As a thought leader, consultant, and practitioner, his experience coaching leaders, developing managers, and designing innovative curricula and pedagogical approaches has prepared him to share insights on corporate learning strategy. His book will benefit large and small companies alike that are proactively preparing for the competitive challenges of tomorrow. The value is rooted not just in the development of a world-class training portfolio, but its integration with key priorities of the business. For companies unfamiliar with this approach, or unsure of its benefits, the book will provide a roadmap to effective change and success. For companies already steeped in an integrated approach, the book will introduce new techniques and validate continued focus for competitive advantage.

Indra Nooyi
Chairman and CEO
PepsiCo

PREFACE

earning to Succeed explores the specific intersection among, and interdependence of, corporate strategy, operational planning, and human capital development. Now, more than at any other point in history, learning is critical for fiscal survival and is the core catalyst for competitive advantage in the dynamic global marketplace.

My motivation for writing on this topic stems from my career, which includes cross-sector and cross-industry experiences that all focused on people as an organization's most significant asset for excellence, change, growth, and sustainability. My executive roles in higher education, management consulting, corporations, start-ups, not-for-profits, and governing boards exposed me to myriad contexts that illustrated both success and failure and provided a breadth and depth of experience that focused especially on maximizing performance and succeeding through the power of learning.

In addition to my professional experiences and active participation as a session instructor/facilitator, executive coach, and P&L manager, I conducted research for this book specifically over the last four years—the period immediately following the global financial crisis. Data was cumulatively sourced through:

- Interviews and focus groups with more than 250 global CEOs, CLOs, and other C-suite executives
- Surveys and questionnaires from over 400 global division heads and business unit managers from large and small companies
- Personal observations of over 500 board and strategic planning meetings, learning and development sessions, and active work environments featuring more than 5,000 global managers and employees
- Discussions with dozens of global academics and thought leaders both to solicit additional insight as well as to validate and collectively analyze data

The themes that emerged from the data helped set the theoretical construct and provide the framework, tools, and recommendations for implementation of a Continuous Integration of Learning and Strategy (CILS) model.

Throughout the book, a series of vignettes and case studies are used to demonstrate key points and illustrate the application of strategic approaches. In most cases, pseudonyms are used to disguise the identity of and protect featured individuals, organizations, and situations. The vignettes, however, represent actual episodes that have taken place in organizations around the world. In addition, actual cases and interviews are also profiled and labeled with the affiliated executive and organization.

In my current role as Chief Learning Officer of Goldman Sachs, I work with senior leadership and managers across the firm to develop and enhance innovative learning initiatives that are aligned with strategic priorities and position the organization for best-in-class product innovation, precision execution, and client service. As with other organizations, Goldman Sachs will consider the best practice recommendations in this book and apply them, as appropriately based, on circumstances and unique needs. Ultimately, the objective for all organizations is to leverage the benchmarked practices to create customized strategies that result in success.

ACKNOWLEDGMENTS

Thank you to the following individuals without whose contributions and support this book would not have been written: Andy Atzert, Mary Ledonne Bank, Susan Beck, Marianne Bellino, Kerryann Benjamin, Geri Bernal, Shannon Berning, Alan Berson, Scott Brooks, Tony Bryk, Peter Cappelli, Craig Carnaroli, Vanessa Carrillo, Dean Carter, Shoma Chatterjee, Barbara Chernow, Paul Choi, Rajeev Chopra, Bart St. Clair, Ian Clark, Lori Collins, Edith Cooper, Phillip Cuffey, Sara Daly, Linda Darling-Hammond, Joe DePinto, Eileen Dillon, Paul Dinas, Alice Duff, Joseph Duff, Charles Dwyer, Ruth Ebert, Erik Evans, Paula Fagundes, Odemiro Fonseca, Eric Foss, Stewart Friedman, Julienne Gherardi, Deb Giffen, Craig Gill, Ken Goldman, Laura Graham, Marty Hackett, Kristin Hales, Ash Hanson, Catherine Hawkes, David Heckman, William Helms, Ken Hicks, Whitney Hischier, Damien Hooper-Campbell, Gordon Houston, Mary Houston, Don Huesman, Lela Wingard Hughes, Govind Iyer, Todd Jick, Sandhya Karpe, Joann Kent, Stephen Kobrin, Michelle LaPointe, Lindsey LaTesta, Mette Laursen, David Levin, Sam Lundquist, Christopher Mason, Lynn McKee, Steve Miller, Robert Mittelstaedt, Bruce

Mosler, Amanda Nelson, John Nixon, Indra Nooyi, Tom Osmond, Mukul Pandya, Alison Peirce, John Percival, Maria Pitone, Georgette Phillips, Lynn Phillips, Sherryann Plesse, Adil Popat, Stephen S. Power, Jonathan Prince, Jason Rabinowitz, Lavanya Ravichandran, Punit Renjen, Kim Ridley, Thomas Robertson, Chelsea Rodriguez, Joe Ryan, Ann Schulte, Greg Shea, Jeff Sheehan, Ken Shropshire, Michael Sivilli, Mary Slaughter, Zach Smith, Martha Soehren, Wendy Sparks, Rajendra Srivastava, Sam Su, Bianca Swift, Claude Trahan, Donald Unger, Michael Useem, Tamela Vieria, John Willig, Edward Wingard, Gingi Wingard, Jaelyn Wingard, Jaia Wingard, Jaxen Wingard, Jazze Wingard, Joye Wingard, Leslie Wingard, Levi Wingard, Marcy Wingard, and Keith Yardley.

Thank you, also, to the following organizations: 7-Eleven; Air Liquide; Aramark; Banco Bradesco; Blackboard; Boston Consulting Group; Capitol Airport Holdings Company; Cheil Industries; Coca-Cola; Columbia University; Comcast Corporation; Crown Prince Court; Cushman & Wakefield; Deloitte; Disney; eBay; Egon Zehnder; Footlocker; Ford Motor Company; Genentech; General Electric; Goldman Sachs & Company, Inc.; Google; Grupo Santander; Haas School of Business, University of California Berkeley; IESE Business School; Indian School of Business; INSEAD; Itau; McGraw-Hill Education; Microsoft; National Football League; Nomura School of Advanced Management; PepsiCo; Philips; Procter & Gamble; Renault; Shanghai Municipal Government;

Sears Holdings; Simbacorp; Singapore Management; Sun Trust Banks; United Nations; Vanguard Group; Wharton School, University of Pennsylvania; Wipro; World Bank; World Economic Forum; Yahoo!; and Yum! Brands.

Introduction

It is clear that corporate learning can have a differentiating impact on performance. However, senior executives need to have a substantive understanding of its uses and benefits, from both a theoretical and practical perspective, in order to fully benefit the process chain.
—Ken Goldman, CFO, Yahoo! Inc., Sunnyvale, California

Companies grow. They change; they mature; and they expand depending on a multitude of dependent and independent variables. Some companies transform themselves in response to such factors as shifts in the marketplace, new technology, new leadership, or new investment partners. What determines the long-term success of any company is its ability to set strategic goals to address the ever-shifting business environment. In order for a company to make the decisions that will ensure its future, a

1

dedication to corporate learning initiatives is essential. For the most successful companies, regardless of size or industry, an ongoing commitment to becoming a dynamic learning organization drives their ability to position themselves ahead of the curve and remain competitive. As W. Edwards Deming wrote in *Out of the Crisis*, "Long-term commitment to new learning and new philosophy is required of any management that seeks transformation. The timid and the fainthearted, and the people that expect quick results, are doomed to disappointment."

The time-honored models for success in any business are changing quickly. No longer can a corporation expect to dominate a particular market by simply creating products to fill a relatively consistent demand and selling them at an acceptable profit margin. In this fast-paced, global landscape, change is the rallying cry of our times. No company can be successful by following the same business model year in, year out. No point on the continuum of current business life guarantees secure revenue, profits, and overall stability. The decision to stand on past triumphs is no longer an option. The future lies in self-assessment and innovation, staying nimble and ready to find solutions to whatever set of challenges arise. In other words, businesses that want to thrive need to become learning organizations.

Learning organizations prosper by addressing the fundamental challenges of the current business world head on. These challenges include the globalization of markets for goods, services, and talent; the acceleration of business cycles, including production, distribution, marketing and capitalization; mounting pressure for demonstrated quarterly return on investment (ROI); and growing competition for market share from companies across the world.

Corporate learning initiatives are the most effective way to meet these challenges. Learning organizations make a commitment to use learning programs for the accumulation and analysis of data to inform major strategic decisions. These programs enable corporate learning programs enable companies to achieve their strategic goals effectively and profitably.

Learning to succeed involves an ongoing commitment to regular evaluation and implementation of corporate programs that enhance the understanding of how the business organization fits into the market in which it operates. From the C-suite to the mailroom, learning initiatives, as configured and supervised by learning professionals within the organization, increase internal communication among segments of the organization, reinforce corporate culture and community, inspire innovation, and increase productivity and profitability. Given adequate resources, well-planned and administered programs will contribute to return on investment in nearly every sector of a company. Once deemed so-called "intangible or soft investments," corporate learning initiatives, training, and executive education have become crucial elements in any company's future growth, competitiveness, and profitability.

The primary concern of this book is to lead managers to a fuller understanding of corporate learning initiatives and how they can be applied to any organization. The goal is to explain that they can work most effectively when integrated into the overall corporate strategic decision-making process. This process of the Continuous Integration of Learning and Strategy (CILS) gives the learning organization the competitive edge in a tough marketplace. Whatever deepens a company's knowledge of the market, competition, and available internal resources enables it to work smarter and benefits the future of the organization.

We are on the cusp of what may be called "The Age of Learning." Innovations in information technology afford us ever newer and more powerful tools to allow for dynamic, multiplatform ways in which to communicate in every segment of the business community. Failure to advance in that direction on the part of individual companies will put them at a severe competitive disadvantage.

Drawing upon the most current information available, as well as examples based on real companies that have reaped the benefits of CILS, this book explains how we can use corporate learning, continuously integrated with strategy, as a powerful and effective response to the problems that buffet global businesses today.

CHAPTER 1

The New Normal

In today's context, organizations are constantly at risk of failing. Using learning as a strategic weapon is not only necessary, but the ultimate tool for competitive advantage.
— Ken Hicks, CEO, Foot Locker, New York

The global landscape for business has changed. Many of the operating models that held true for generations no longer apply in the fast-paced world of contemporary commerce. From day-old startups to centuries-old brands to the new giants of information technology, the impact is the same: Survival requires keeping up with the pace of change. Any business that wants to win has to exceed that pace.

While the depth of the transition of current business thinking is in flux, the warning signs have been out there for decades. Twenty years ago, in the *McKinsey Quarterly*, William W. Lewis, Hans Gerbach, Tom Jansen, and Koji Sakate, wrote:

> Whether in the food industry in the U.S. or the auto industry in Japan, managers and engineers do not arrive at . . . innovations because they are smarter, work harder, or have a better education than their peers. Rather, they do so because they must. They are subjected to intense global competition, where constantly pushing the boundaries of productivity is the price of entry — and of survival.

Is survival the new success? For an increasing number of global companies, the question is not where they will land in the rankings of their industries on an annual basis, nor whether profits will rise or fall. It is whether they will simply fall out of contention *completely*, either as a result of wholesale failure or because their business is subsumed by a more successful global competitor. It is getting harder and harder for companies that need to stay ahead of the competition in order to maintain their market share each year. Cheaper, bigger, faster, and newer are the goals that drive business more than ever. Strategic planning, coupled with an acute knowledge of the markets, keeps companies competitive. Attention to customer service in this age of instant feedback through social media bolsters growth. Responding to change quickly and effectively is vital to survival.

In order to keep pace with change, smart companies depend on communication and information management. Staying on top of best practices in their industry and instituting them effectively in their organizations gives them an edge. Regular reevaluation of in-house systems and personnel in light of market shifts helps prioritize the distribution of resources and increase profitability. Clear, concise, and efficient training initiatives strengthen the communities of the organization and maintain increased productivity and innovation. For any business organization to be successful, it needs to be an organization that *learns* from both its own mistakes and successes, as well as from those of its competitors.

Corporate learning is the key to success in today's data-driven, hyperintegrated world.

New Business Environment

What are some of the most powerful forces in today's business environment, and how can corporate learning help businesses overcome the challenges those forces pose? How can learning organizations harness these forces to their advantage? The answers to these basic but important questions require knowing what the forces are and how they affect the current business environment (see Figure 1-1).

Expanding Global Market

Reach and Structure. A new, highly competitive global reality is dominating the business marketplace. For the first time in history, companies are facing tectonic shifts in the competitive landscape, as the pool of potential resources, strategic partners, customers, and competitors expands dramatically.

No longer can businesses expect to "own" a regional or domestic market to which they provide products or services. Cheap garlic from China has all but replaced the domestically grown garlic that used to dominate kitchens throughout America. Quintessential brands, such as Goodyear and IBM, must now compete for market share with competitive products from Asia and South America.

No longer can companies rely on the dominance of a centralized corporate structure in one of the commercial centers of the developed world. Companies seeking global reach must have large satellite offices in major markets throughout the world. The top six accounting firms have offices in every major financial capital. Information giants, such Google and Microsoft, have expanded their presence to meet competition in growing markets in Asia. Retail conglomerates, such as Amazon and Walmart, have operations throughout the globe.

No longer is competition confined by geography. Communications technology, Internet marketing, and increasing efficiencies in distribution channels enable any company to compete globally. A marketing strategy firm

- Evaporating Regional Boundaries
- Multipoint Operational Presence
- Common Language Denominator
- Cultural Awareness and Sensitivity
- Digitally Sourced Efficiencies
- Mergers and Strategic Partnerships

Global Market Shifts

Business Cycle Variability

- Constricted Production Timelines
- Socio-Political Conflicts and Force Majeure Events
- Market Needs Assessment and Gap Analysis

- Short-Term Profit Emphasis
- Optimized Productivity Expectations
- Long-Term Planning Sacrifice

Return On Investment Focus

Business

Figure 1-1   Dynamic Business Enviroment

in London may see competition for domestic customers from agencies in Mumbai, India, or Lima, Peru. That same firm may form a new partnership with a social media provider in Auckland, New Zealand, to secure business with a retail chain in Cape Town, South Africa. Manufacturing takes place in remote areas of the globe, often closer to the source of raw materials or processing plants. Globalization of both management and service has become the new standard. Learning to adapt to global expansion through structural alignment and outreach is critical to gaining a competitive advantage.

Communication and Culture. In the past, one of the obstacles to entering new international markets has been how to communicate ideas, proposals, and strategic directives to clients, vendors, and partners. With the advent of high-speed methods of sending information around the globe and the pervasiveness of Western business and cultural practices, a common language needed to be adopted. That common language is English, and it serves to facilitate global business. While many companies still rely on local languages to communicate with indigenous workers, managers, consumers, and business associates, global communications concerning business is, for the most part, conducted in English.

Increased understanding and acceptance of cultural differences and similarities that help professional relationships to flourish have replaced parochialism. Decades of global travel, media, and education have opened up the world and all but closed the chasm among disparate markets in ways that we have never before seen. Instead of viewing regional behaviors or patterns as problematic, people now view those as part of daily business practice, altering their own behavior accordingly as a sign of respect and mutual interest. Americans who work or conduct significant business in Asia routinely have business cards with English on one side and Japanese or another

Asian language on the reverse. Business must take cultural practices into consideration. For instance, during the month-long Chinese New Year festival, over a billion people leave their jobs to travel to visit family in rural China. This annual mass migration has the effect of virtually shutting down normal supply channels vital to international business. As a result, businesses that rely on China for goods and services must build this holiday into their ongoing business plans. Learning to leverage communication and culture for competitive advantage is critical.

Technology Bridge. As businesses diversify and decentralize their operations to meet globalized demand, they depend on technologies to manage and support dispersed enterprises. Recent advances in Internet communications allow for virtual meeting environments, complex transactions and secure information sharing, and collaborative project management and work-flow solutions. Computer programming and logistics algorithms are enabling more efficient physical transport of goods and services. This further minimizes the disruption created by distance. Simulation and modeling software are able to realistically demonstrate concepts so that the inability to connect live is not an issue at all. As a result of these and other advances, the list of activities that require short radius accessibility is dwindling.

The chief operating officer of a large, Atlanta-based manufacturing conglomerate previously relied on a local blue chip financial accounting firm with which they had been working in partnership for decades. However, as a result of advances in communication technology and the pressure to control costs and secure maximum value, she now has the option to work simultaneously with companies in New York, Chicago, Toronto, and England. Through the use of leading-edge technology and programs, all of the company's transactions can be aptly managed remotely—from meetings to iterative document review to animated analysis and projection report demonstrations. Learning to leverage technology for competitive advantage is critical.

Decentralization and Consolidation. As the expansion of global markets continues to accelerate, any company that wants to maximize revenue must reset its sights on clients and customers they never would have imagined existed in the past. Socioeconomic factors, such as the explosion of the middle class in India and China and its appetite for Western goods, have brought new business to companies, large and small, throughout the developed world. Kopenhagen Fur, the largest auctioneer of mink pelts in the world, is dominated by merchants and manufacturers from China seeking to meet the growing demand for luxury fur coats. Global professional services in the legal and accounting sectors are expanding to meet the needs of multinationals doing business around the world as well. Even top-tier American universities are expanding their brands and revenues by setting up satellite campuses around the world.

Over time, these trends have caused an unprecedented number of companies to hire and maintain decentralized workforces. As these companies have broadened their geographic footprint, the nature and rate of transactions and engagements with global partners has also increased, resulting in, among other shifts, the increased incidence of mergers, acquisitions, and strategic partnerships. All of this aggregation has helped to further develop the sophistication of modalities that enable companies to do business around the globe. Multinational companies, while based in one location, now have operations and personnel all over the world. Each of their hubs creates a separate network of professional relationships suitable for conducting business in that locale.

A chemical company from Rio de Janeiro that specializes in plastics recently acquired a company in Wilmington. Management teams, staff, vendors, and partners were deployed to both cities. In time, the "blending" of cultural approaches, transaction standards, and strategic operating methods created a C-change in the basic structure of the organizations—one that now teaches local approaches and seeds another crop of global opportunities . . . and competitors. The proliferation of companies, like this one, expanding globally has given rise to even greater boundary busting. Learning to leverage networks for growth and competitive advantage is critical.

Shorter and Unpredictable Business Cycles

Time-to-Market Pressure. The competitive arena initiated by global expansion has specifically influenced time-to-market pressures and revenue-to-profit cycles. The sooner a company gets a product on the shelf or unveils a new service methodology or is able to respond to a complex RFP, the more likely it will be able fend off competitors and survive. These shorter cycles, however, put significant pressure on an organization. If a company's business plan, operating schedule, and production system are not equipped to consistently accelerate cycles, then the stress of keeping pace with competitors is overwhelming and, ultimately, the company's plan becomes impossible to implement. Operating within the comfort zone of the company's infrastructure and system may not be an option in today's fast-paced commercial climate. The constant pressure to decrease the time-to-market of new products and new versions of existing products requires that businesses integrate time-saving and efficiency-improving technology and methodologies of product development and marketing. Learning to leverage new systems quickly to shorten production to delivery schedules is critical for maintaining a competitive advantage.

Market Forces Disruption. In today's global economy, sociopolitical events affect the entire business community more quickly and deeply than ever before. Conflict in the

14

Middle East can disrupt the slow transport of crude oil, making prices higher and impacting the bottom line of thousands of companies. The disastrous flood in Bangkok in 2013 forced the temporary closure of 17 factories, disrupting the global supply chain for high-tech products for weeks. Fluctuations in global currencies, the growing problem of sovereign debt in emerging markets, the regulatory requirements and their impact on the introduction of goods and services in foreign markets all contribute to the volatility of doing business globally.

Unexpected or uncontrollable market forces can also wreak havoc on planned business cycles. A pharmaceutical firm in New York had to postpone its release of a hallmark new drug because of delays in receiving patent clearance from the U.S. government. The government's delay was based on litigation issues associated with a clinical trial for a different drug, but nonetheless, it impacted the approval schedules of both. In real time, international competitors with less government regulation filled the gap in their local markets.

Fluctuations in global currencies, dramatic swings in global stock markets, and devastating *force majeure* and related emergency weather events can all cause significant disruption in the new business environment. All too often, organizations are not prepared to deal with these events. Combined with the fact that the global nature of today's business practices exponentially affects the potential effects of sudden and unexpected market forces, many businesses are on a collision course with failure. Learning to develop flexible systems to respond to unexpected scenarios is critical for competitive advantage.

Shift in Market Demand. In today's complex environment, most companies engage in some form of analytical demand-based testing before developing and marketing their offerings. Even when this is done, the proliferation of parallel and competing offerings being introduced into the marketplace and the constant shifts in client/consumer needs create constantly changing targets. In other words, doing business is increasingly a guessing game to determine *what* the "next big thing" will be and *when* it will be in demand. To tackle this issue, companies are faced with two main options:

1. Produce a wider portfolio of products or expansive suite of services to increase the likelihood that something you have developed will match the sweet spot of demand.
2. Take your best guess at the "killer solution" through careful assessment and planning and hope that it hits the mark at the right time.

Most companies do not have the resources to "hedge their bets" by blanketing the market with a wide tapestry of offerings. So, they take the risk, however calculated they would argue, and aim for the "sweet spot." Learning to develop enhanced analytical protocols and gap analysis systems is critical to stay competitive.

Increased ROI Pressure

Return Expectations and Shareholder Anxiety. A key corollary to the unprecedented acceleration of business cycles is the unprecedented pressure companies face for faster and stronger returns on their investments. Traditional business models were designed to achieve financial goals within an annual fiscal period. The increased emphasis on short-term profits, often measured from quarter to quarter, from boards of directors and increasingly more aggressive shareholders, have forced CEOs to adjust their strategic planning.

In an era of such unprecedented and intense competition, companies need more immediate and stronger returns on their investments. Cost-cutting to meet top-line financial goals and enhanced productivity strategies are leading priorities for large and small companies in the postrecession climate. The pressure has created an environment where most companies cannot withstand down cycles in their performance. This has implications for historic approaches to investing in longer-term planning to maintain competitive advantage over time. In the short term, cash flow may be at risk if revenue slides and new products do not take hold. Additionally, shareholder anxiety tends to hover in a continuous, watchful loop given the unpredictability of quarterly earnings, putting the strategic allocation of resources and reinvestment alternatives at risk. Working lean means doing more with less, forcing organizations to reevaluate the way they do business.

Short and Long-Term Priorities. Without investments in long-term planning, sustained growth, and solid profitability become difficult to achieve. It is a delicate balancing act, but both are necessary. Companies need to maintain a commitment to the growth of their futures, even in the face of the aforementioned intensity of short-term pressure, while at the same time developing tools that ensure sharp and timely assessment and analysis that leads to innovation and market competitiveness in the daily cycle of business.

As efficiency and ROI pressure remain the primary goals of large and small firms alike, the focus on reducing operating costs and optimizing workforce productivity become the short-term strategies that overshadow any long-term objectives. Gone are the days when an organization can comfortably manage and absorb the ebb and flow of cyclical returns and expect to win now and in the future. Learning to execute short-term priorities for ROI while still forecasting and planning longer term priorities is critical for competitive advantage.

New Priorities

While the specific goals vary by industry and within separate companies, the new priority is clear: Align resources to achieve more with less to support aggressive quarterly profit expectations. The intense competition of today's hypercharged business environment, with its constant focus on ever faster ROI, has prompted companies to react by focusing on two specific and related strategic directives: precision execution through performance management and precision investment focused on functional and personnel priorities.

Precision Execution

Business Planning. It is an accepted rule of business that that every wasted dollar is a dollar that takes away from an organization's bottom line. In the present climate, business leaders scrutinize resources with greater urgency. When a company is under competitive assault from every corner of the globe, it engages in systematic analysis and development. The most obvious and available way to improve returns is to improve productivity. And precision execution—operational excellence that employs minimal outlay for maximal yield—is the key to improving productivity. Well-managed business planning processes can allow units to succeed in spite of this challenging environment. The critical first step in business planning is setting priorities first for the corporation, then for its specific organizational units, divisions, or teams.

This may sound obvious, but the new business environment has no tolerance for nonspecific alignment of objectives to resources. The "no-fluff" factor forces managers to be explicitly specific with respect to areas of focus. Once these priorities are deduced, budget planning follows. Allocating financial resources to each area is often a painstakingly laborious process, particularly when there is not enough money to fund the pool. To achieve this goal, successive rounds of prioritization are required. Staffing, technology upgrades, research and development, facility upgrades, and marketing and sales outreach are among the most significant budget items. Questions and discussions often include:

"Given all that we've been asked to do this year, how many additional head count can I expect?"

"My team is already stretched to the maximum limit. Since everyone is functioning outside of their job scope, how much of an increase [in compensation] can I give my people?"

"Now that we have two new long-term contracts in Munich, we should put a junior associate on the ground. The time difference and time to travel are counterproductive."

"How can we possibly achieve our goal if we lay off 10% of our team this cycle? Rehiring them later will cost more in the long run."

"We're in desperate need of expertise in the area of systems integration. The lack of personnel in this particular area is costing us business."

In addition to staffing and personnel, considerations about outsourcing are also critical:

"Should we hire a full-time manager or engage an agency for an initial six months?"
"Since the R&D mandate may only last this year, we should consider hiring a firm and redirecting the team toward higher priority projects."

After the budget has been set, a template for tracking and measuring success should be developed and implemented. Since adherence to budget limits is necessary, regular updates and careful monitoring of the plan helps ensure progress. This is particularly important if the plan is managed better than expected and surplus funds can be redirected to new target areas that have emerged. In the event that projects have taken the budget over the limit, it is important that corrective procedures be put in place—before critical deadlines. Learning to operationalize a sound business planning process and manage change with defined and prioritized boundaries is critical for competitive advantage.

Performance Management. Directing, motivating, and measuring the impact of individual employees collectively contributes to the operational efficiency equation. All staff feel the effects of needing to perform at the highest level. In a nutshell, performance management is a formal system that provides objective and subjective data on a given employee—as measured against goals, peers, and group/company performance. The primary components include:

- Communicating expectations
- Goal setting
- Commercial execution and results
- Feedback
- Learning and development
- Recognition and rewards

A key ingredient in the performance management process is that managers clearly communicate and articulate overall expectations to the team. This is a platform for translating company strategy and priorities into team priorities. Once team members understand the overall company direction, focus, and desired results, it is easier to make sense of individual unit expectations. Further, reinforced messaging continues to link work to higher order objectives and reminds staff why their work matters and how it connects broadly throughout the organization. Learning through targeted programs to communicate corporate expectations enhances performance at all levels.

Goal setting for individual employees becomes critical when the broader messaging has been delivered. Outlining specific expectations for what each person is being directed to achieve leaves no room for ambiguity about how an employee should be spending his or her time, allocating resources, or prioritizing projects. As a result, teams can achieve maximum efficiency as individuals engage in direct activities.

Often, in addition to basic goals, "stretch goals" that require an individual to either extend beyond the scope of their current position or extend beyond their current skill and capability set have become part of the planning process. To meet these goals, development opportunities are needed to prepare that individual to close the gap on experience or ability to meet his or her goals. Learning and development play a pivotal role in complementing the goal-setting process.

A primary component in the performance management cycle includes commercial execution—or getting work done! Meeting, and hopefully exceeding, result expectations is the overall desired outcome. Assuring that the complementary performance components are in place is necessary for the ongoing delivery of high-level results. In other words, people don't just show up and perform at a high level; they need a process and support chain that is the framework of the performance management system.

Ongoing feedback from managers provides a formal mechanism for assessing progress against a tight performance schedule, as well as recalibrating any adjusted expectations that have evolved during the review period. Again, performance management is often leveraged as a reaction to competitive pressures. The feedback process maps progress against expectations at various points in time and redirects when needed.

The drive to compete and succeed breeds internal intensity, as people are generally working harder than they expected they would. Providing outlets for recognition and reward goes a long way toward maintaining levels of commitment and engagement. When positioned as part of the performance management process and tied directly to clear, well-defined milestones, incentives can produce stellar results. The approach minimizes miscommunication about expectations concerning performance. Learning to enhance precise execution practices through business planning and performance management overall results in greater efficiency.

Precision Investments

Perhaps the most aggressive strategy companies use to react to the changing business environment is the targeted investment of capital in prioritized categories of operations. Investments in functional areas include technology and marketing. Relational areas include people (staff) and vendors, customers, and clients. The investments are used to directly enhance market position in the face of increased competition.

Functional. Technological investments in software and systems upgrades, communication platforms, enhanced mobile devices, and hardware replacement all close the gap on competition created by global expansion, cycle reductions, and ROI pressure. Although spending on new or upgraded technology may, at times, seem excessive during cycles of tight budgets, the solutions they create actually justify the expenditure through greater efficiency of communication and systems management.

Investments in marketing help a company shape and promote industry profile and product offerings. When consumers and clients have an increasing number of companies and products to choose from, reminders of who is out there and what they do becomes a critical positioning tool. From traditional billboards and brochures to bleeding-edge social media platforms, smart marketing can tip the scales in the competitive arena. It is important to note, however, that content and positioning drives marketing campaigns, so a company's clarity with respect to its target audience, message, and response strategy is very important.

A glass manufacturer in Chicago had been steadfastly losing market share to a group of competitors in Mexico City. Price was, in large part, the reason for the initial shifts in business. The Chicago-based company streamlined its operations and brought down its price. Then, it employed aggressive sales and marketing efforts to highlight its competitive position. The targeted investment, although an upfront outlay, recovered the previously lost share and revenue.

Relational. Investment in professional relationship building is always controversial. As the business environment changes in a way that makes the work environment less attractive, a focus on the culture of and investment in employees is a shrewd if somewhat "soft" strategic move.

When people are motivated, they work harder. When a cultural environment at work is positive, energetic, and hopeful, then productivity soars. Small tokens of appreciation, such as free snacks, dedicated lounge areas, flexible work arrangements, or sponsored holiday parties, can go a long way toward reengaging employees. Investments in corporate learning initiatives for professional development and organized community building create a workplace that is both supportive and aspirational, even if compensation is flat. Whatever the approach, a focus on employee health, development, and/or happiness goes a long way toward fueling a motivated, committed, and productive workforce.

Similarly, company focus on its vendors and clients has a dramatic effect. From customer appreciation days to increased client field visits, special attention directed to this base signals, along with ramped up client services, demonstrated appreciation for their business. In an age where protecting the client base is increasingly more difficult, mining the existing pool and giving them additional reasons to remain connected is vital. Learning to direct investments to targeted functions and populations in a company's professional ecosystem make a big difference in contributions to the bottom line.

New Strategic Partner

The changing business environment has caused companies to respond with new priorities to fend off competitive pressures and realize competitive leveling. For ultimate growth, success, and survival, corporate learning initiatives as a partner to strategic planning have the greatest impact on the health and future of any business organization.

Classic Approach

Supplemental and Separate. Corporate learning encompasses a wide range of functions and formats. Historically, it has been used as a mechanism for rewarding high performers, for remediating poor performers, or preparing targeted groups for new roles and responsibilities. Its primary function has been to help shape and support the strategic goals of the company by creating dynamic ways to communicate these goals and the programs designed to facilitate their achievement. These include such programs as high-potential training, executive education, coaching, client consultation services, analytics, and benchmarking. At best, corporate learning initiatives have consistently underscored the need for every corner of an organization to remain open to new information and models to increase efficiency.

Offering Sequence. Even the most effective corporate learning programs are often introduced *after* (or separate from when) strategic goals are decided. In a business environment driven by an increasing need to remain current and flexible, corporate learning initiatives need to be part of strategic planning *from the beginning* to better serve the needs of the organization (see Figure 1-2). CEOs and

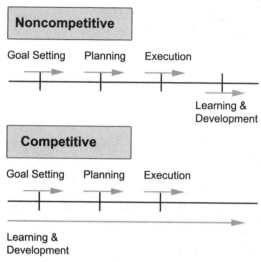

Figure 1-2 Directive for Offering Sequence

their boards need to recognize that the value of corporate learning is a key element in any long-term goal for the organization.

Process Shift

Strategic Codependents. Dynamic changes in business impact how companies adjust their operating strategies to remain relevant so they can compete on the global stage. Corporate learning offers a powerful tool for building strategic goals and articulating how they can be accomplished, and then implementing targeted programs to achieve them. Cojoining strategic planning and corporate learning initiatives is fundamental to the shifting of a company from a static to a dynamic learning organization.

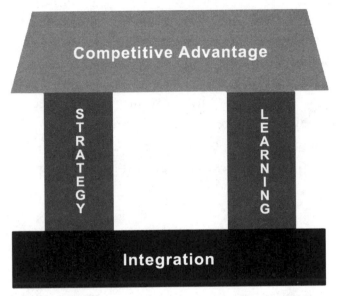

Figure 1-3 Continuous Integration of Learning and Strategy (CILS)

CILS as Vital. Corporate learning is an organization's most important strategic partner (see Figure 1-3). Any effective corporate strategy targets its key internal and external stakeholders and how they fit into the long-range goals of the company. Given the market conditions and resulting impact on the business and its people, corporate learning helps define critical strategic priorities (ones that are at once aggressive yet achievable) and simultaneously serves as a principle catalyst for, and driver of, the implementation of that strategy. When paired with the strategic planning process from the beginning and used to complement and carry out the initiatives of the strategic plan, a company is uniquely prepared to not only compete in the new market economy, but to succeed.

The CILS process defines the relationship between strategic planning and corporate learning as fundamental partners. This consistent, constantly evolving collaboration during every step, from strategy development through implementation and back to redevelopment, is vital to contemporary businesses, large and small, for two major reasons:

1. Ambitious strategy development consistently risks formulating priorities and plans that are too disconnected from the reality of what can actually be achieved in an organization. Corporate learning initiatives, built on an integrated framework and deep knowledge of all aspects of the organization, serves as an invaluable "reality" check regarding the creation of practical strategic goals.

2. Complex strategy implementation is based on the effective organization and utilization of resources. Corporate learning offers a detail understanding of how to allocate resources cost effectively to make the stipulated goals a reality. In today's hypercompetitive global environment, missteps are costly and lead to loss of market share or failure. The level of sophistication required to create a well-coordinated and continuously accessible platform of development and preparatory resources is what CILS brings to the table.

Summary

The global business environment has evolved into a highly competitive arena where companies of every shape and size face unprecedented challenges from competitors around the world. Traditional business models are crumbling, while new models are constantly evolving. Quick return on investment expectations compete with long-term financial planning and growth tactics. Change and speed are the new status quo. Keeping up with the pace of change gives an organization a competitive advantage. The best corporate leadership understands that getting ahead of the change curve is the only way to thrive.

Advances in information technology contribute to the globalization of markets. Socioeconomic, commercial, or political events in one corner of the global can affect business tens of thousands of miles away. With English as the dominant language for most business transactions, there are fewer and fewer barriers to communications. "Exotic" cultural practices that once obscured doing business have become part of the normal day-to-day routine.

There simply is not room for mismanagement or wasted resources in today's business environment. Two of the most effective methods to achieve maximum returns are precision execution and precision investments. Both of these approaches require insight and assessment tools that enable long- and short-term strategic planning. Information acquisition and analysis coupled with a deep knowledge of the industry and the internal systems of an organization are vitally important to the future.

Companies looking for a competitive advantage must rely on corporate learning to provide the data tools necessary to set strategic goals by employing the CILS model.

CHAPTER 2

An Integration Formula

Workplace learning needs to be woven into the fabric of an organization and not viewed as an after-thought. If done right, it helps the organization retain knowledge and stay ahead of changes impacting our field.
—Ian Clark, CEO, Genentech, San Francisco

The Continuous Integration of Learning and Strategy (CILS) is the key to long-term business success. The leadership structure in companies can vary according to their size and complexity. Large and midsized companies are usually organized in a hierarchy that includes officer-level leaders, such as Chief Executive Officers (CEO), Chief Financial Officers (CFO), Chief Operating Officer (COO), and Chief Learning Officer (CLO), as well as a Board of Directors that guides the fate of organization in tandem with these executives. Smaller companies often have a less stratified leadership, in which the members of management team share responsibility for in all aspects of company with or without a formal Board of Directors. Regardless of their size and organizational structure, all companies have two things in common: growth through profitability and the need for information to help them achieve these goals.

As already discussed, the business environment continues to become more complex and faster paced. The need for current information about market shifts, new technologies, and financial opportunities is paramount for survival and success. Gathering that information, processing it, presenting it clearly and concisely to management, and then creating strategies that shape the goals of the company and the systems to achieve them is the foundation for success. In larger to midsized companies, this function is usually the responsibility of the Chief Learning Officer in conjunction with Human Resources and other departments. In smaller companies, without the organizational resources and personnel to designate this significant role to executive level divisions, the gathering of information is done on an ad hoc or even an event-driven basis by various members of the management team. For instance, market information might be acquired by the sales and marketing leaders, and financial information by the business managers.

However, no matter what the internal leadership systems are, there will always be the need to address the initiative of CILS. Since this function is fundamental to the health of all companies and involves similar objectives, I will refer to its administration and application as being handled by *the office of the CLO*.

Over the past two decades since Jack Welch reportedly coined the term and supported the executive level position of Chief Learning Officer ("Taking Work-Place Learning to the Next Level," *Knowledge@Wharton.upenn.edu*), large companies have introduced this position to head corporate learning, training, and executive education. As the need for information and corporate learning initiatives grew, the importance of the office of the CLO began to have an impact on the overall strategic goals of the organization. However, the traditional business model for companies continues to relegate the functions of the office of the CLO to a supporting role in the overall administration of business. Whether it is the C-suite of larger companies or the scrappy founder of a smaller company, these leaders often consider CILS a "soft" function that is often difficult to implement and even more difficult to quantify in terms of impact. Allocation of funds is often problematic and not always sufficient to achieve a complete and dynamic CILS program. As result of this long-held idea, the office of the CLO has not been included in the strategic planning of the company.

In order for a company to transform into an active learning organization, its management needs to recognize the benefit of the integration of corporate learning initiatives into the long-term strategic planning of the company. In larger corporations with the resources to support the position of Chief Learning Officer, the best way to advance this approach is to make the CLO part of the official C-suite. In smaller, less complicated companies with fewer institutional resources, senior management needs to reorient its priorities and task senior managers with exploring and proposing learning initiatives early in the strategic process. The reason is clear: The learning initiatives, as developed by the office of the CLO, are critical to the representation, advocacy, and oversight of the learning segment of any company's strategic goals. By virtue of the information gathering process and the analysis and implementation of initiatives through internal systems, the office of the CLO is in the best position to create a long-term vision of achievable strategic goals and how to reach them.

Mapping an Organizational Profile

Integration Formula

For a company to implement CILS, its management needs to follow a specific integration process. The elements of this process constitute a formula that, when instituted in sequence, creates a path to developing an integrated learning organization poised for maximum competitive advantage. Simply, the effective CILS formula may be described as:

> *Quadrant Profile Mapping*
> *+ Structural Foundation*
> *+ Content Components*
> *+ Assessment/Alignment/Execution*
> *+ Evaluation*
> _____
> *= Continuous Integration of Learning and*
> *Strategy (CILS).*

While the configuration of the elements in the formula may vary depending on the size of the company and its approach to corporate learning, the basic formula remains effective.

Quadrant Analysis

Before this integration process can occur, a company needs to take stock of how it has traditionally balanced corporate learning initiatives with the overall decision process of setting long-term goals and organizational culture. Without a deep understanding of these relationships, it is difficult for any corporate entity to move forward effectively with the implementation of the CILS process.

Quadrant analysis is a simple way to assess the organizational role that learning initiatives play in any company. It serves to unpack broad portfolios of activities and transforms dry data into a diagnostic tool. By taking into consideration corporate culture, customer ratings, market penetration, growth, innovation and a variety of other factors, quadrants create a snapshot of the fundamental nature of how a company balances learning and strategy.

Gathering the data on which to base the quadrant profile need not require a labor intensive audit of every single aspect of an organization. General information can be gleaned from past budget allocations to learning initiatives, an understanding of what the programs entailed, and an awareness of how closely they were connected to the strategic goals set. Mapping a profile involves two basic, parallel assessments. First, what kind of strategic planning process does the organization employ? Does it favor short-term over long-term strategic planning or vice versa? Are priorities easily articulated? Has a business planning and execution approach been tied to each priority?

Second, how comprehensive is the company's suite of learning initiatives? Are they organized more as a string of stand-alone efforts or are they grouped into structured categories? Are these initiatives tied to strategic priorities? The process of evaluating a company's past approach to corporate learning and the established goals will result in an understanding of what quadrant the company falls into. Once mapped, companies learn what their current attitude toward the integration of learning and strategy is and take the appropriate actions to move it forward.

With this information gathered, it is not difficult to use the quadrant analytic tool to create a basic profile of where a company fits on the spectrum of becoming a learning organization.

Corporate Learning Application

Figure 2-1 highlights four potential combinations that define the relationship between a company's strategic planning and its learning initiatives. This analysis tracks the evolution of a company from its early stage through mature development. Quadrant One represents start-up companies that have no long-term strategic planning or learning initiatives. Quadrant Two represents first-stage companies that have long-term strategic goals, but no learning initiatives in place. Quadrant-Three companies are in second-stage growth and have long-term strategies but only basic learning initiatives. Quadrant Four highlights mature companies that have evolving long-term strategies and integrated learning initiatives.

Wherever the threshold is set, companies eventually reach a level of operational complexity that requires a com-

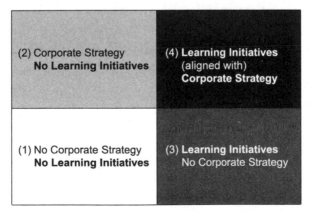

Figure 2-1   A Taxonomy of Company Positions

mitment to CILS. The examination, analysis, and adjustment of both corporate strategy and corporate learning are not event-driven activities to be used in response to a particular problem. Quadrant Four companies make it an organizational priority through the alignment, integration, and deployment of learning initiatives tied to and, continually adjusted to, corporate strategies. Taking concerted steps to transform a company into a Quadrant Four organization represents the most advantageous approach to competing and succeeding in the present business environment.

Structural Foundation

To begin the process of integrating corporate strategy with learning initiatives, management needs to recognize the imperative of transforming its company into a *learning organization.* According to Peter M. Senge, whose book *The Fifth Discipline: The Art & Practice of the Learning Organization,* was one of the first to articulate the importance of integrating strategy and learning, states "... [learning] organizations where people continually expand their capacity to create the results they truly desire, where new and expansive patterns of thinking are nurtured, where collective aspiration is set free, and where people are continually learning to see the whole together."

Components of Aligned Strategy

Quadrant Four companies have the greatest potential to become successful learning organizations. As such, the company values the pervasive role corporate learning plays in strategic planning and understands how to achieve it through CILS. One of the most important steps in the process is attention to the structure of the organization, specifically at the executive level.

Executive Alignment. Senior management needs to recognize the viability of the learning function and initiatives as an integral part of the strategic planning process. As the main proponent and administrator of the learning initiative, the office of the CLO needs to included on that senior management team, reporting directly to a primary decision maker—be it the CEO, president, or a founding partner. This organizational shift in approach is the critical structural foundation that will ensure that CILS has ultimate buy-in and, therefore, success (see Figure 2-2).

Once the office of CLO is included in the executive decision-making process, it is positioned to participate as a genuine strategic collaborator. This means that the people in charge of learning initiatives must have a strong, active, and significant voice in activities, such as priority setting, decision making, and resource allocation. This structural change in the role and position of the office of the CLO in an organization may be seen as contrary to the status quo. Traditionally, this position has fallen under

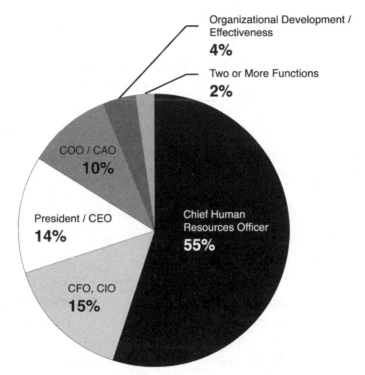

Figure 2-2 CLO Reporting Relationships

the aegis of Human Resources because it involves programs that target all levels of personnel from leadership
development to training and onboarding procedures for
managers and non-managers alike. As of this writing, more
than 50 percent of CLOs in large corporations do not
report to the CEO or president—either directly or dually.
Most report singularly to the head of Human Resources.
This structure is indicative of an approach to corporate
learning at all levels of the business community.

As pressure mounts in the competitive global marketplace for faster, more market-driven information to inform corporate planning, the office of the CLO has taken on an increasingly crucial role in the overall success of a company. As a result, more corporations are elevating this position to the executive suite or its equivalent.

All consequential learning is based on programs of teaching, training, and communication. In the context of any organization, the primary target and consumer of these programs are its employees—from the senior executives to the rank and file. The office of the CLO is then tasked to create and administer these programs.

Consistent with the evolving nature and complexity of the office of the CLO is the growing trend to include that person on the executive team. This reflects the expanded role the CLOS has in developing corporate learning initiatives, which encompass a wide variety of significant sectors that contribute to a company's success. The office of the CLO or its equivalent is responsible for keeping the company informed about external market forces and changes, the shifting needs of vendors and clients, the internal culture adjustments required to address systems and operations, and new technologies that impact the creation and implementation of learning programs. The acquisition, presentation, and analysis of this information through the office of the CLO contribute to solid long-range strategic plans.

Its role extends to monitoring and evaluating the company against other peer and cross-industry organizations.

All stakeholders need to remain aware of the company's leadership in learning and development. Senior management needs to know, on a continuing basis, that the resources applied to learning efforts have allowed the organization to keep pace, or extend beyond, what others are offering their employees. New recruits and existing employees also need to understand how the learning function compares to what is offered at other places. Proactive benchmarking allows the office of the CLO to monitor the product and service offerings partly based on knowing what others are doing and seeking to outpace them.

For an organization to integrate strategy with corporate learning, there needs to be a shift in the roles of the offices of the CLO and Human Resources. To use a military analogy: The office of the CLO needs to be part of the mid-to-long term *strategic* planning of the corporation, while Human Resources needs to take on the equally important *tactical* role of coordinating and implementing the programs that will achieve shorter term goals that support the strategic ones. The is analogous to the Joint Chiefs of Staff, in which the Commander in Chief (CEO) consults with his cadre of Cabinet-level officials (COO, CFO, CLO), each of whom contributes to the strategy for winning the war. Once the strategic battle plan is determined, the Chairman of the Joint Chiefs (HR) takes over to assign the resources necessary to get the job done.

Several dynamics become clear in this schematic of management and corporate learning. It is important for the offices of the CLO and Human Resources to report

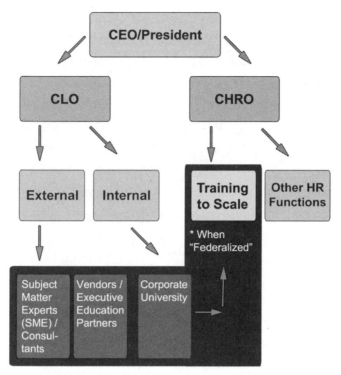

Figure 2-3 Authority over Learning and Development Resources

directly but separately to the CEO, president, or senior executive. This allows them the authority over their considerable and significant areas of specialization and focus. These lines of authority can also facilitate the "federalization" or temporary reallocation of resources when necessary to achieve company-wide goals, such as training personnel or educational programs.

While the specific areas of supervision differ with the size and nature of each organization, the general breakdown of responsibilities remains similar. For instance, an organization might not be as large as McDonalds or Disney or Lufthansa. Therefore, it may not warrant an in-house, permanent "university," at which employees and managers are trained. The office of the CLO needs to be responsible for the learning initiatives that will affect the strategy of the company-at-large in whatever form is best for the corporation. The office of Human Resources, working with the CLO, needs to be responsible for employee management, as well as the construction and implementation of the agreed-upon programs.

Content Alignment. Accurate and up-to-date information, both internal and external to an organization, fuels CILS. As information experts, learning professionals are the primary resource for the accumulation and analysis of content. This content flows through numerous channels, including reports on past performance, industry journals, blogs, social media outlets, and the personal experiences of employees, vendors, and clients.

Corporate learning as a general term comprises myriad different methodological approaches to the dissemination of significant content throughout an organization. Individually, each component plays a part in helping to satisfy specific learning objectives for a targeted need. Collectively, they form the fabric of a true learning organization.

Every organization needs to adjust the components to its specific needs. Once the strategic goals are set, the office of the CLO is responsible for sorting through the options and linking them to the achievement of designated deliverables. Traditional learning is live (in-person), classroom based, and set against a time boundary from a few hours to a few days or weeks. Experiential learning includes customized simulated modules, role plays, on-the-job structured demonstration enactments, and field experiences. E-learning is an umbrella term for a digital platform that includes online/web-based instructional programs, massive open online courses (MOOCs), and simulated games. Mentoring, apprenticeship, executive coaching, and management consulting satisfy specific performance outcomes through flexible, direct engagements.

Content components and methodologies should be tailored to specific learning goals. Many of these programs and curricula are highly specialized. Their content design and development is often best accomplished by subject-matter experts (SME), who specialize in and contribute the specially crafted content for learning that internal personnel then administer. These experts are often outsourced from vendors to help approach the initiatives at hand. The SMEs have deep expertise in targeted areas or across topics, and they provide thought leadership and thought partnership in the development and delivery of learning experiences across types and platforms. Instructional designers may work in close concert with SMEs and are charged with defining learning objectives, creating programmatic curriculum, selecting delivery types and channels, and customizing materials to an intended audience.

Corporate learning professionals make effective use of other potential content development and management partners as well. These include internal human resource professionals who serve as liaisons between lines of business, units, or teams, and specialized corporate service centers, which may include experts in government relations and compliance, corporate communications, and legal affairs. They facilitate the exchange of business needs to the subject matter experts and designers to ensure that objectives are properly aligned and addressed. Outsourced consultants can fill a variety of roles as well. Faculty and specialized speakers are adept at using engaging (and sometimes entertaining) presentation skills to convey concepts and content to audiences across platforms. Executive coaches help to collect feedback on employees from subordinates, peers, and other stakeholders, providing coded (or themed) recommendations for behavior. Business school experts often help design and coordinate executive education and training programs. Custom programs are designed specifically for teams of managers at a specific company—usually with company-related projects built into the curriculum.

Leadership Role

In order for a company to transform into an active learning organization, the CEO and the Board of Directors need to recognize the need for a senior learning executive to be part of the C-suite. These executives are critical for the representation, advocacy, and oversight of the learning part of the "integrating learning and strategy" equation.

Title Variability. The titles for these learning executives vary depending on organizational size, structure, and evolution in professional development activity and focus. Whatever the title, this role needs to be exclusively focused on learning and development, as opposed to being bundled as an add-on responsibility of another role, such as the Chief Human Resources Officer. Without exclusive focus and learning and development, an executive will be unable to drive a CILS agenda for success. A few sample titles for of learning executives include Head of Learning and Development, Senior Vice President of Talent Management, and Global Director of Training and Organizational Development. The title of Chief Learning Officer is presently the most widely used and is accepted as the signatory for the senior-most individual responsible for learning, training, and leadership development. As such, I will largely use this title in the discussion.

Goal Setting and Priority. In the CILS process, developing a strategy requires setting goals. These goals, in turn, require the gathering and analysis of different types of data (internal resource data, market analysis data, skill gap assessment, etc.). One of the key responsibilities of the Chief Learning Officer is to distill this information from up and down the information chain and present it in the context of the decision-making process. The CLO can help shape these goals by providing valuable input concerning viability based on talent status and company resources. As the central coalition builder of any organization, the CLO coordinates all stakeholders, both internal and external, through communication of corporate goals and the related programs set up to help meet or exceed them. For example, if a company's strategic goal is to increase the diversity of its leadership pipeline, the CLO can be a valuable stakeholder in the process by:

1. Understanding and/or conducting assessment profiles of top performers across the targeted population categories
2. Designing and offering development programs for that population to prepare for future opportunities
3. Facilitating the identification and selection of "ready" candidates and their transition into promotion roles
4. Providing ongoing coaching and other leadership support resources to ensure candidates are successful

In this example, it is clear how the link between a strategic priority and connected learning initiatives needs to be integrated for successful implementation.

Learning Team and Vendor Management. The CLO is responsible for managing a learning team and external vendors who, when combined with this team, provide the infrastructure for carrying out a CILS approach. As discussed, this infrastructure is comprised of a variety of components that collectively make up a learning franchise. The CLO's leadership responsibility in managing the franchise depends, again, on the size and evolution of the company. Large companies that have been focused on learning and development for an established period typically have a leadership development center of excellence and a corporate university. These units are often led by a learning executive or a CLO. The leadership development center is essentially focused on the senior executives of the company. Given the unique responsibilities of senior executives, specialized initiatives need to be crafted that cater to their areas of need. These include, but are not limited to, managerial effectiveness, succession planning, stakeholder communications, and board governance. The corporate university is an internal construct that houses development activities for the rest of the company's populations—from entry-level new hires to mid-managers to junior executives. Topics covered in the corporate university range from technical skills training to business team planning facilitation. Both the leadership development center of excellence and the corporate university staff create initiatives with internal subject matter experts and project managers, as well as external consultants, coaches, and training organizations, such as business schools.

Small to mid-sized companies that have focused on learning and development for a more truncated period of time typically have a different organizational configuration than large companies. As leadership authority for the function is usually assigned to a Chief Human Resources

Officer, whose primary activities usually include internal coordination between a human resources generalist or business partner and the business division. Occasionally, a training manager resource is available to partner with the generalist to design and deliver programs for the company staff or to outsource programs to training vendors.

Company Ambassador. As the resident learning expert, the CLO owns the role of company ambassador. Part of this responsibility is to use the leadership platform to broadly and continuously articulate the value proposition of the need for, and benefits of, learning and development. Businesses are full of managers and individual contributors who are solely focused on the task at hand—producing products and services better and faster to win the competitive race. As such, no one is usually focused on the support mechanisms that help to get this work done.

In the case of learning, the CLO can articulate the value proposition so that (1) staff know and understand what development resources are available, how they can be used, and what are the expected returns; and (2) success stories are properly communicated and shared through the organization as evidence of adoption and practical impact. Highlighting success and impact is particularly important because fast-moving businesses and their people require constant reminders of why time should be taken away from the principal task at hand (the work) to engage in activities (training) that "might" help them directly in the future.

An operations vice president of an insurance agency recently oversaw a massive round of layoffs in his department. Following a resurgence of demand in the business, he was forced to hire back the 25 percent of the staff he had released just 18 months ago. The high percentage of new employees satisfied the headcount requirement, but did not replenish the loss of institutional knowledge. The VP initially considered engaging the corporate university to help develop a custom curriculum for the new hires, but he was concerned about further reducing his production output by taking workers away from their jobs to participate. After hearing a series of success stories from his CLO about how similar situations had been improved or solved by targeted development initiatives, he chose to proceed after all. In this case, the success and impact profiling proved beneficial.

In addition to the value proposition and the success story messaging, the CLO's role as an ambassador also extends to monitoring and evaluating the company against other peer and cross-industry organizations.

It is important for several stakeholders to remain aware of the company's leadership in learning and development. The board and senior management peers need to know, on a continuous basis, that the resources applied to learning efforts have allowed them to keep pace, or extend beyond, what others are offering their employees. New recruits and existing employees also need to understand how the learning function compares to what is offered at other places. Proactive benchmarking allows the CLO and his or her team to (1) continuously innovate product and service offerings partly based on knowing what others are doing and seeking to outpace them; and (2) use the message of relative superiority, when appropriate, as an advertisement of competitive advantage.

Thought Leader and Practitioner. In addition to management responsibilities, the CLO is expected to be a thought leader in the learning and leadership development space. As a content expert, he or she should write about new research, best practice approaches across functions and using different methodologies, and lessons learned from direct implementation. This content can flow through numerous channels, including journals, blogs, social media outlets, and trade magazines. Teaching is a channel for sharing best practice content. It may include lecturing in workshops, facilitating training sessions, presenting at conferences, delivering keynote addresses, moderating panels, or coaching individuals and small groups. (see Figure 2-3). Although the CLO of a large organization may have the resources of internal staff and external consultants to teach internal programs, they must also engage in this exercise to:

1. Maintain current and sharp practitioner skills.
2. Remain connected to the needs and expectations of the workforce.
3. Strengthen relationships with internal clients from the business units.

4. Understand the nuances of the development experiences to help with the management and development of other teachers.

Performance Management Monitor. The final role of the learning executive or CLO is monitoring performance management. Performance management is whatever process an organization uses to ensure that goals are being met by staff and individual contributions are being evaluated. It is important for an organization to ensure that performance management in the organization follows basic components of a development cycle (see Figure 2-4).

First, managers need to set and communicate expectations for their teams. Second, they need to set and communicate specific goals to individuals. Although both are obvious, research shows that employees are unsure of group direction 20 percent of the time and of individual expectations 15 percent of the time. Third, a learning and development plan needs to be established for individuals

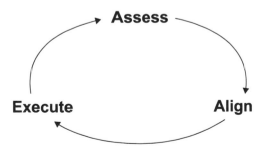

Figure 2-4 Full Cycle Integration

to (1) provide support for stretch goals that require enhanced development and training and (2) address skills gaps in individuals whose performance has them on notice or probation. Fourth, rewards in the form of positive recognition or compensation should be given based on objective criteria that are linked, mostly, to the original goals.

It is the CLO's responsibility, in particular, to monitor the performance review process and specifically focus on learning and development as an ongoing lever in the process. Absent the performance management process, learning and development in organizations remains untethered to the core function of the business. Embedded between goal setting and rewards-based evaluation solidifies it as a significant cog in the cycle of performance.

CEO Sponsorship

Essential to the structure of CILS is ensuring that the CEO and/or president provides required sponsorship of the learning function and initiatives and actively participates in their implementation in strategic ways.

Role Addition and Inclusion. First and foremost, the CEO should advocate for, and fully endorse, the inclusion of a learning executive or CLO role in the C-suite. For the reasons discussed, adding the CLO as a member of the C-suite is a critical structural foundation, and the top-down endorsement ensures that CILS has ultimate buy-in. This important step signals that strategy will be influenced by learning considerations and alignment opportunities.

"Real" Strategic Collaboration. After ensuring the CLO role is included, nominally, in the executive ranks, he or she must then be positioned to participate as a genuine strategic collaborator. In other words, the CLO's affiliation with the group must be real! This means that the CLO must have a strong, active, and significant voice in activities, such as priority setting, decision making, and resource allocation commitments. A nominal appointment would, in contrast, allow the CLO to only lead learning and development initiatives *after* the primary C-suite executives had already made the principle strategic decisions for the business.

> "In their book, *The Chief Learning Officer,* Tarnar Elkeles and Jack J. Phillips argue for the CLO's strategic positioning and function in the organization. They wrote: "The learning and development department is often involved in developing the strategic plan for the organization. In this role, the CLO has a 'seat at the table' where strategy is developed and provides important input, raises critical issues, voices necessary concerns, and offers suggestions and solutions to share the direction of the learning function. This is perhaps the most critical role of learning and development in its linkage to strategy."

Resource Allocation. In order for the necessary learning initiatives to truly align with their strategic priority counterparts, the CEO must, again, advocate for the CLO to work in partnership with the rest of the C-suite on resource allocation. We know that alignment, in and of itself, is not enough to influence success in initiatives. It takes money, people, and time. It is part of the CLO's role not only to identify learning matches for priorities, but to also make sure that the proper level of resources is allocated to do it the right way. If the CEO consistently provides a chair for the CLO at the proverbial resource table, the foundation for CILS will remain sound.

Participant or Teaching Role. When the CEO participates in learning programs, it sends a very strong signal to the rest of the organizational community that learning is valued and integral to the success of the business. In some cases, a cameo appearance by the CEO during a class, conference, or other program is all that is necessary. In other cases, momentum is derived from the CEO participating more formally as a presenter, panelist, or interviewee. Further, CEOs can demonstrate support for the function by leveraging opportunities for themselves such as coaching or reverse mentoring.

Take the example of Ali, the president of a prestigious college near London. In recent years, the college was under fire amid a flurry of accusations and convictions of assault cases on campus. The negative impact on public perception and diminished safety on campus resulted in a

20 percent enrollment decrease over a two-year period. The loss in tuition revenue jeopardized funding streams to elective outlets, including the radio and television studio, health and wellness center, and newspaper.

A cross-departmental committee was charged with developing a strategic plan to raise awareness, establish protocols, and enhance overall campus safety and security. The complementary objective was to bring the college back into good financial standing.

To signal the importance of the learning and communication effort and to mobilize immediate action, Ali hosted a series of evening "teach-in" meetings, held outside and featuring bonfires. The setting allowed for unlimited participation and encouraged efficient agendas. The weekly series, which lasted the duration of the fall semester, provided Ali with a platform to educate faculty, staff, and students on the issue, allow them to tell stories and voice concerns, and answer prevalent questions with candor and reassurance. As the leader of the organization, his active role in participating in the development initiative provided buy-in and relevance that would have otherwise been difficult to obtain.

Communication Agenda. A CEO's communication platform is broad and powerful. The CEO's leveraging of that platform for key messages related to and supporting learning as a strategic tool and differentiator further allows the CILS process to work. Announcements or mentions by the CEO at all-staff meetings are likely the most effective all-encompassing way to signal the value of learning to the company. With limited time available for such meetings, time blocks are precious real estate. So, one can believe that anything mentioned during those meetings is a high priority and definitely *not* merely tangential to the business. In these cases, the CEO can also tag-team with the CLO to highlight topical highlights or simply give the CLO time to speak directly (as a CFO would take a few minutes to present on financial forecasts). Additional channels for communication that the CEO can leverage include all-staff memos, divisional presentations, and mentions in all forms of media. A CEO of a small apparel retail chain in Copenhagen conducted a virtual all-staff meeting to give 10 key strategic updates affecting the company at the midpoint of the year. For each, he not only profiled financial and competitive opportunities and challenges, but he also laid out learning initiatives for each that were or would be supporting integration.

Manager Modeling and Integration

Demonstration of Lessons in Practice. If CEOs take the lead in supporting the role of the CLO and the comprehensive uses and functions of learning, it sets the stage for all managers in the organization to do the same. Divisional and line managers have an opportunity to demonstrate learned lessons in practice. For example, they may have recently learned leadership lessons on topics such as "communicating constructive feedback," "creating an apprenticeship culture," or "integrating work and home." For each, they can demonstrate learned best practices and new patterns of behavior to improve their business and validate how the learning initiatives can make an immediate difference in workplace performance. Further, referring to our discussion on performance management, the managers can use their own development as a primer setting expectations for how they want the team to learn to behave and perform.

Stretch Assignments and Development. As previously discussed, managers can demonstrate success of, and adherence to, learning initiatives as agents of change for stretch assignments. How did a technical engineer in Des Moines prepare to serve as project lead for a major, 100-person team, multimillion dollar government contract when she had never before managed even *one* person? The answer is that she and her manager collaborated to create a development plan that included competencies in project management, team efficiency practices, and specialized groundwater reclamation procedures. After an intensive development preparation experience, she succeeded beyond and in spite of her experience parameters.

Culture of Development

Proactive Accountability. The last rung on the foundational structure ladder holds the weight of individual responsibility and an embedded overall culture of development. Once an infrastructure for learning has been established, led by a learning executive with direct access to, and participation in, the strategic direction of the company, then it sets the stage for managers to model and expect learned behaviors of excellence. From there, the whole company should be inspired and bought into being part of an engaged community of applied learners. A true learning organization has central and cascaded support, but it also thrives on proactive accountability from all of its members. If learning is valued by the company and staff alike, if it is expected to be available and to work, then it will permeate the culture and solidify the foundation that requires strategy to be reinforced by active and insatiable learning. Staff in a company should not only participate in sponsored programs, its members should also learn to seek their own development opportunities through alternative outlets.

For example, one might take a course online after work or attend a conference during work that they found on their own. In either case, using professional development experiences to broaden knowledge in a way that either directly benefits their job performance is critical to building a corporate culture of engaged thinkers and inquirers who are actively pursuing support for questions, challenges, or deficiencies in their repertoire of skills and their knowledge. This makes the buzz of intellectual energy in the company more electrifying.

Valued/Expected/Rewarded. In addition to filling their own bucket of learning experiences, corporate culture is enhanced by collectives of individual members "reaching back" to contribute to others' development through such activities as mentoring, apprenticing, or technical advising. These, too, push the work environment to realize greater excellence with ideas, strategies, and innovation tactics, all fueled by a support foundation and culture of learning and development.

For example, Luis oversees a flight control command pod for an airport in Lima. After 29 years of service, Luis has benefited greatly from an apprenticeship culture that nurtured his development and allowed him to learn the nuances of his job, as well as the broader context of the whole operation, through direct, hands-on experience and individual support from peers and direct superiors alike.

Luis also gained from joining the organization when it was a small airport servicing 20 to 30 flights per day. Now, following significant expansion and growth, the airport services hundreds of flights per day covering a landing area that is 30 times the size it was when Luis started. Further, the profile of the airport has changed from regional to international. Safety regulations dominate, and often cripple, the operational process, and the race to keep pace with technological advances often requires creative solutions for alternative execution. Luis' experience in all of these areas serves as a valuable resource for a staff that averages only seven years of tenure and for an organization that has grown too fast and too large to provide the same type of apprenticeship culture that provided Luis' foundation.

To contribute to and support a culture of learning, Luis holds office hours twice a week. These working lunches provide opportunities for his more junior colleagues to discuss case scenarios that they have recently encountered or are in the middle of solving. Following a framework that includes both mentoring and technical assistance, Luis asks guiding questions, provides relevant historical examples, participates in "whiteboard" and brainstorming sessions, and, in some cases, works beyond his office hours to shadow the employee as they execute in real time on the job. These efforts not only model learning, both giving and receiving, as a responsibility in the organization, but also contribute to maintaining excellence as the cultural environment experiences dramatic shifts.

Integration Elements

Assessment

In the CILS process, developing a strategy requires setting goals. The CEO and members of the senior leadership team first need to be armed with a clear vision based on an accurate assessment of the landscape. To achieve this, they need to be willing to commit to capturing:

1. An accurate assessment of the company—both its strengths and its weaknesses
2. An accurate assessment of markets—both current and potential

To be a full partner in implementing this strategic vision, the office of the CLO must be able to acquire information about how things work and assess what is functional (and what is dysfunctional or simply suboptimal) at every level of the company. These goals, in turn, require the gathering and analysis of different types of data, including internal resources, market analysis, and skill gap assessment data. One of the key responsibilities of the CLO is to distill this information from up and down the information chain and present it in the context of the decision-making process.

The initial assessment cycle is vital to the success of the integration of strategy and learning. Accurately assessing a company's current profile is relatively straightforward. For the most part, it involves gathering and collating various information streams, including costs and profits, markets, and competitors. As the central coalition builder of any organization, the CLO is uniquely positioned to assemble data that will serve as the basis for that assessment. In larger companies with a CLO and team in place, this is done by the creation of fact-finding programs, surveys, interviews with key employees and managers, and overall data sharing and observation. Once the data is accumulated, the CLO and his or her group can put together an accurate profile of the company's current operations and effectiveness. Once this data is available, the long-term plan for integrating corporate strategy and learning programs becomes a reality.

In smaller companies that do not have this internal structure and access to resources, the process becomes a team effort, with every division contributing to the acquisition of data. While there might be a senior manager who is responsible for coordinating the methodology and process, the actual work might be done on a decentralized basis, with each department creating a report on its specific area for the senior management team. These reports might be presented by the individual managers or digested by the manager coordinating the effort. The senior management team can then base its strategic planning goal on the information the data conveys.

It is important to remember that this data is critical in shaping goals by providing valuable input concerning their viability based on talent status and company resources. For example, if a strategic goal of a company is to increase the diversity of the leadership pipeline, the office of the CLO can be a valuable stakeholder in the process by:

1. Overseeing the assessment profiles of top performers across the targeted population categories
2. Supervising the development and implementation of development programs for that population to prepare for future opportunities
3. Facilitating the identification and selection of "ready" candidates and their transition into promotion roles
4. Providing ongoing coaching and other leadership support resources to ensure candidates are successful

Companies with an established CLO structure might outsource some of program development work. Smaller companies would rely on hands-on managers to help find the best ways to target and support the potential of workers within these diverse groups based, on the employee reviews and practical knowledge of the systems as they exist.

> "An organization is ready to be a learning organization when it can accept criticism and is willing to learn from others. It is willing to be critical of itself and is as interested in how to improve what it did well as what it did poorly."—Ken Hicks, CEO, Foot Locker, Inc., from "Running Man: Foot Locker Chief Leading Rare Retail Turnaround." *Forbes Magazine*, August, 2012

Alignment

Once the company sets support of CILS as a top priority, the value proposition of the need for, and benefits of, learning and development shares the center stage with other key initiatives. The ultimate goal is to move toward the alignment of all resources and stakeholders in the CILS process.

Businesses are full of managers and individual contributors who are solely focused on the task at hand— producing products and services better and faster to win the competitive race. As such, no one is usually focused on company-wide learning initiatives that help to get the work done. Designating CILS as key a component in the executive decision-making process can lead to better communication of the importance of learning programs to the staff, helping them understand what development resources are available and how they can be used to further their goals. Therefore, highlighting success and the impact of learning initiatives is particularly important. Fast-moving businesses and their employees require constant reminders of why corporate learning is worth the investment of the time taken away from their principal responsibilities.

Aligning learning initiatives with their strategic priority counterparts requires valuable resources in capital, personnel, and time. Understanding the potential importance of alignment to the company is not enough to support the success of CILS. The office of the CLO must not only identify learning matches for strategic priorities, but must also make sure that the appropriate level of resources is allocated to get the job done.

Execution

Once the assessment is made, the resources allocated, programs planned, and alignment with goals established, the final piece of the formula is execution. Together with Human Resources, the office of the CLO supervises the implementation of learning initiatives. Whatever the size of the company, this process usually begins with the managers. They are fully briefed on the programs linked to their particular teams. Once they are on board, they set and communicate expectations for their team and their individual reports—specifically highlighting the educational resources available to bridge skills gaps necessary for execution.

The offices of the CLO and HR monitor the execution and often are called on to provide support for stretch goals that require enhanced development and training and to address existing performance gaps in individuals. For instance, Oscar is the chief administrative officer of a theme park outside of Paris. Facing increasing competition from other regional attractions and a reduction in entertainment-based consumer spending, the board decided to double down and focus on the customer experience as a key differentiator to regain attendance numbers.

Message mandates of service were cascaded throughout every department in the park, and individual goals were weighted strongly toward customer relationship metrics. In cases where employees did not have direct exposure to customers or where interaction was limited, specific skill development was mandated. For each staff member, customized competencies for quality customer service were charted against his or her skills to determine gap levels and develop a plan. After four years of overseeing the execution of the learning and development program, Oscar's organization not only survived its decline in ticket sales, but realized a 41 percent increase in independently audited customer satisfaction reports.

Evaluation

For any CILS initiative to be successful, it needs to be monitored continually for effectiveness and adjustment. In creating learning initiative programs, the office of the

CLO must incorporate a mechanism to evaluate their success or failure. In large companies, there is usually a team within the office of the CLO to monitor existing programs. Once the learning initiative programs are up and running, the office of the CLO receives regular reports on their progress and impact. Once this evaluation is complete, adjustments are made to increase the effectiveness of the programs. In small companies, the oversight and evaluation of learning initiatives are less formalized (see Figure 2-5).

Eva is the Global Head of Human Resources for an investment bank based in Hong Kong. The multinational bank has recently finalized the settlement of two acquisitions, infused capital into the operating budget to align with targeted growth priorities, consistently outperformed expectations and delivered dividends to shareholders, and positioned itself for near- and long-term expansion by gaining the majority share in two select, specialty market areas. The firm, however, is simultaneously entangled in multiple lawsuits related to governmental policy issues and vulnerable to resource constriction associated with these external distractions.

To respond to new regulatory and compliance requirements and to prepare for more frequent and aggressive auditing and legal missteps, Eva's firm decided to prioritize the development of an organization-wide training initiative. The target audience would be everyone in the organization—from top to bottom, including board members, key consultants, and temporary staff.

Given the significance of the investment outlay and the urgency to regain control of organizational behavior, Eva was charged with leading a process that focused on a cycle of design and redevelopment. The concept for the training was based on a strategic priority that maintained top-down and complete organizational support. Following the typical design and delivery of a suite of programs leveraging multiple platforms, Eva's team outsourced the collection and analysis of impact data. The consulting firm reviewed attendance, participation levels, assessment (exam) performance, and contribution to job-specific goals. The analysis leveraged both quantitative and qualitative data to assess the relative impact of the training and was then used to revisit the design and adjust accordingly. The cycle of turnaround was noteworthy in that it was monthly, and the redesign levels in the first 18 months averaged 50 percent—meaning the course curriculum and/or

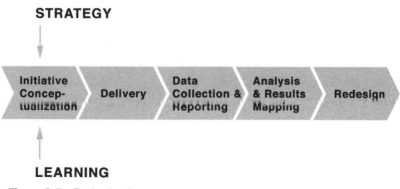

STRATEGY

Initiative Conceptualization — Delivery — Data Collection & Reporting — Analysis & Results Mapping — Redesign

LEARNING

Figure 2-5 Evaluation Process

methodology was changed at a significant level multiple times and relaunched in new form quickly thereafter.

In addition to modeling organization-wide commitment to the integration of learning and strategy, Eva's firm showcased how an effective evaluation process can allow the development initiatives to evolve to a maximum impact level in an extremely truncated timeline.

Summary

Continuous Integration of Learning and Strategy (CILS) is key to the success of any company, regardless of size. Upper management's support of this initiative is critical if it is to have the desired impact on the long-term goals of the company. To administer this important directive, a company needs to establish the position of Chief Learning Officer. In large companies, a designated CLO is responsible for this ongoing initiative. In smaller companies, this significant function is usually handled by a variety of managers often in conjunction with Human Resources.

Once the supervisory infrastructure for CILS is established, its success requires that all senior management support it. Unlike old models, in which learning initiatives were viewed as general information and training programs only tangentially related to the general corporate goals and installed after they were decided on, these initiatives must be on the ground floor of all strategic planning. Once granted direct access to, and participation in, the strategic direction of the company, the executives responsible for the office of the CLO can effectively use resources to propose programs that will help managers and employees achieve corporate goals. From there, the whole company can be inspired to work together as part of an engaged community of applied learners. A true learning organization has central and cascaded support. This shift in the traditional organizational structure is the critical initial step in the process of full and effective integration between corporate learning and strategic planning.

The steps or elements in the Integration Formula accelerate the process of creating an effective CILS program. They include understanding the key components available to create and support the learning initiative; the active role and responsibility of the office of the CLO or its equivalent to assess, align, and execute the learning programs; and finally, the evaluation of the effectiveness of the program. In line with the goals of transforming a company into a dynamic learning organization, this formula serves as the basis for introducing and maintaining a thriving CILS program.

If learning is valued by the entire company, and if everyone expects it to be available and to work, then learning must permeate a company's culture. It must also solidify the foundation that requires strategy to be reinforced by active and updated learning. Once staff members are used to participating in sponsored programs, they will also learn to seek their own development opportunities through alternative outlets. Whether these experiences broaden knowledge in a way that directly benefits their job performance or not, it is critical to building a corporate culture of learning and development.

CHAPTER 3

A Programming
Framework

*A balanced and methodologically innovative portfolio of
offerings truly distinguishes a corporate learning function —
and ensures that it directly benefits the bottom line.*
—Rajeev Chopra, CEO, Consumer Luminaires, Philips,
Brussels

For corporate learning to be an integral part of a company's strategic path forward, it should <u>not</u> exist as a collection of training events or activities strung together by time and place, an ongoing reaction to Just-In-time requests from key stakeholders in the business, or a catalogue of courses or topical menu of programs. Rather, all initiatives in a corporation's arsenal of offerings should be mapped against a framework that organizes and categorizes them in such a way that the ultimate purpose—supporting strategy development and execution—is optimally fulfilled.

Once mapped to a framework, learning initiatives should then be consistently evaluated to ensure that they are following a [assessment → design → implementation] process for quality control and impact.

Channel and Method Components

A useful framework for corporate learning is based on the three foundational pillars of Thought Leadership and Insights, Development Programs, and Advisory Services (see Figure 3-1). Each pillar contains a collection of com-

Thought Leadership & Insights

- Convenings
- Content Development
- Sourcing
- Outreach

Development Programs

- Cohort Groups
- High Potentials
- Targeted / Strategic Shifts
- Clients

Advisory Services

- Assessment
- Consulting
- Coaching

Figure 3-1   Three-Pillar Approach to Building a Learning Framework

ponents that should, in aggregate, comprise of the total portfolio of a company's learning initiatives. Put simply, if a proposed learning initiative *doesn't* somehow map to this framework, then it shouldn't be included! Ideally, however, a company should endeavor to have initiatives in each of the three categories. A heavy imbalance signifies that the learning organization is underleveraging the power of a dynamic mix of opportunities. Understanding the types of initiatives that fall into each pillar is useful in determining how to organize a complete learning organization.

Thought Leadership and Insights

This category of programs and initiatives is often overlooked as fundamental to an integrated strategy. But, in fact, it is quickly becoming the most critical component in the learning agenda of global companies seeking to provide employees with new knowledge. It includes new information, resources, and tools—gleaned from research, best practices, or personal experiences—across topic areas. It is extremely important in today's context, as the shift to a complex global economy requires that individuals become resourceful knowledge workers, who demonstrate a broad understanding of a wide range of topics and consistently feed themselves with useful and varied nuggets of new information. These insights become relevant, in practice, as problems in the workplace require solutions that are based on a broad understanding of a tapestry of topics.

Convenings. One way companies can introduce general insights to staff is through functional convenings. Gatherings of groups of people are an ideal way to introduce almost any topic area and take learning to scale very quickly. Conferences, summits, forums, roundtables, and interview panels are methods of convening that companies can use to expose participants to management and operations topics, such as:

1. Strategies facing women in global government leadership roles
2. Lessons in teamwork best practices from the orchestra
3. Advice on organizing and establishing sustainable work-community partnerships

Again, while some of these topics do not appear to align directly to any company's core business or functional skill need, the expanded knowledge base of employees *is* critical for not only personal fulfillment and development, but also for breadth of awareness and insights on various approaches to work and life that are directly applicable to business objectives and role expectations. Since convening formats can be extremely flexible, the development opportunities can be tailored for specific audiences. Thought leaders may include university faculty, government leaders, sports and entertainment leaders, and corporate executives (external or internal).

Convenings can take any number of forms, depending on the resources of the company and the goal of the program. No matter the size or format, the result of any information exchange is always to create an atmosphere of continuous learning and dedication to innovation and improvement.

Smaller companies without the resources to sponsor large-scale convenings can achieve similar results thorough more targeted gatherings. The CILS coordinators might organize regular meetings to share pertinent updates and best practices with departmental managers, who then communicate this information to their reports. Periodic updates over coffee and donuts for employees or similar information "brown-bag seminars" are another way to keep thought leaders energized and driven to create.

For larger organizations with deeper budgets, company-wide convenings often are the best way to approach this goal. Multinational corporations frequently combine physical and virtual meeting formats to share information and energize their teams.

An aeronautics and defense company conducts an annual conference on "Materials Rollout" where it profiles all of the new metals, plastics, carbon fibers, and other materials that are being introduced to produce new equipment. Over the course of two days, every employee has the opportunity to learn about the various materials and their application to the overall business. The purpose is simply to teach staff, from across divisions and up and down the seniority chain, how one particular aspect of the business works. In return, the company asks employees to reflect on how the learning experience might positively affect their respective roles. Facilitated by the office of the CLO, the learning initiative has proven to increase correlated productivity by 7 percent. In the case of this learning initiative, exposure to new knowledge, combined with reflection and application, results annually in changed behavior and positive results.

Content Development. As we enter the postinformation age, it is becoming increasingly clearer that we can never have enough information at our disposal. Content is king and should anchor the office of the CLO. Indices and benchmarks are tools that can be used to organize useful data for learning. Good and relevant content supports the goal of thought leadership. However, how can managers and employees be expected to sort through the morass of information available? Depending on the size and resources of a company, learning professionals often serve as the reliable source of information that will prove useful to a company's efforts. In large corporations with a dedicated CLO and staff, the learning professionals aggregate the huge amount available information related to the industry, marketplace, and workplace. After sorting through the massive data at their disposal, the learning managers help select, distill, organize, and present the most relevant information to the company and its employees regularly.

For instance, there are reams of information concerning the best practices for the acquisition of new business in any given industry. These best practices are constantly shifting in response to changes in regulations, market forces, and developments in technology. Large corporations rely on the office of the CLO to employ its expert knowledge of the operations of the corporation to sort through this information. One large financial services company has developed a "Top-10" index of reports of action primers for areas of interest, such as "ways to re-attract lost customers" and "key market trends that lead to spikes in sales performance." The learning professionals distribute these reports, which are based on the learning experiences and data provided by other organizations, throughout the company and support them with targeted convenings to address specific questions. It is a complicated and expensive process, but it reaps great rewards by keeping every member of the organization well informed and competitively prepared.

Smaller companies face a greater challenge in addressing the constant flow of information. Without the help of a well-funded, dedicated team of information experts working closely with the learning professionals, it might not be possible to digest the information most relevant to the needs of the company and its staff on an ongoing basis. One approach these companies take is to access the information available at industry association meetings, which are usually held annually. At these conventions, the newest trends and information are often revealed and digested at presentations by vendors and industry spokespeople. A small company might send one or two representatives to a convention, who are responsible for gleaning information that might influence the company and then report back to the staff. Another approach might be to designate someone in each department to check on the primary sources of industry information, usually available online on dedicated websites, on a periodic basis and share any news with their department by email.

Another powerful method to deliver applied content is benchmarking, or the process of aspiring to a standard of excellence in any given field. Comparing similar processes, such as attrition rates, standard cycles between research development and production, and rehiring timetables of other companies, provides the basis for thinking about strategies for improvement in the parent organization. In larger companies, this kind of in-depth analysis is usually performed by the office of the CLO and presented to aid in the strategic planning process. In smaller companies, benchmarking might take a more informal approach. Because they do not have the resources for detailed research and analysis, key personnel in the company, from top management down, keep their ears to ground concerning what is happening both in the business community and in their industry and report on how current trends can be applied to the organization.

Today, content can be distributed through a variety of channels. Articles, white papers, reports, and books are traditional channels, while blogs and social media represent newer interfaces. In either case, publishing content and distributing it to both internal and external audiences showcases the company's strong thought leadership platform and depth of content—specifically as it relates to learning and leadership development.

A technology company in San Francisco developed an interactive learning blog that was moderated by internal staff of the corporate university. Every week, the blog profiles a new development topic related to operations and management fields (finance, legal, compliance, human resources, etc.). Within one quarter, the blog participation rate had reached 75 percent of the company. Employees commented on approaches to development and learning, provided examples of efforts in practice, recommended design considerations, and recognized observed success in the workplace. As a learning tool, the blog engaged a wide audience in an ongoing dialogue about how acquiring knowledge can impact business. As a thought leadership forum powered by expert- and participant-generated content, this initiative shows why it should be mapped to the overall learning framework and that its effectiveness is not nontraditional, but simply unique to this category of programming.

Sourcing. Distributing thought leadership content through live, in-person conferences and forums has high design value and can often scale to fairly large audiences. However, for maximum scalability and accessibility, an asynchronous distribution approach is even better. "Learning portals" are specialized company intranets that can house content and offerings for the whole learning function, but, in particular, are appropriate for showcasing thought leadership and insights content.

Successful, high-level executives in any organization have accumulated a great deal of expertise in their field. Many have become respected spokespeople to whom members of the business community rely for accurate information and insights. By creating a source for pertinent information using internal thought leaders, learning professionals can leverage this expertise to promote learning programs inside the company. In addition to keeping the company on its toes and current, sourcing has the residual benefit of helping create a sense of community of mutual development and support.

An office retail products company in Buenos Aires routinely interviews its executives for perspectives on management and success. The company also interviews external leaders to get exposure to, and compare, alternative best-practice approaches. In both cases, the videos are recorded, digitized, and housed on the learning portal. Employees then have access on demand to the source videos, which are sorted by topic for ease of identification. Trends indicate that up to 50 percent of the organization views each interview within 30 days of posting. The sourcing of the content in this way ensures the breadth of impact of the initiative by penetrating an otherwise hard-to-reach audience.

Outreach. In some cases, organizations take the opportunity to share their best practices, insights, and thought leadership with external audiences. Whether it is a reciprocal arrangement, civic duty, or a perception-building purpose, companies have extraordinary amounts of data and information that can be shared. Once again, this is not historically considered learning, but it does fall into the thought leadership and insights pillar of the learning framework because developing individuals or groups of professionals inside or outside of the organization to support strategy is the essence of the CILS objective. Keynote addresses at dinner galas, presentations at conferences, and structured interviews and opinion pieces with targeted media outlets highlight just a few of the outreach channels where the office of the CLO can coordinate the dissemination of thought leadership outside of the company.

Outreach is a way of using company experts to promote the company as an industry-wide thought leader. Learning professionals help coach these experts as public speakers, then work with their public relations partners to get them high-profile engagements, such as keynote speakers at industry meetings or interviews in business media. Many believe outreach efforts to be the hallmark of business public relations in the future. The higher the stature of its thought leaders, the higher the profile of the company becomes as an industry leader. These outreach efforts attract new talent and new business to the company as well.

In the case of organizations known for innovation and a creative approach to product development, sourcing through corporate leaders can achieve the same results without a great deal of capital expenditure or coordination.

In the early days of Apple and Microsoft, their respective CEOs, Steve Jobs and Bill Gates, became the visionary experts in the burgeoning field of personal computing. At the time, their companies were small, struggling to promote a new kind of computing to consumers and industry insiders alike in the face of well-established competitors like IBM. In their positioning as industry experts, they communicated new concepts that eventually grew to become the norm, revolutionized the industry, and made them the giants they became.

Development Programs

Professionals are most familiar with learning initiatives in this category, as they are most clearly aligned with traditional corporate training. It is important to remember, however, that a smorgasbord of basic, stand-alone training offerings is not an effective structure to accomplish CILS. What is needed are organized designs for targeted populations based on a foundational learning framework. These designs need to include a mix of contemporary designs and methodologies to be successful with distinct populations.

Cohort. Every company develops a unique network of distinct employee communities inside its general organizational structure. Each of these communities, or cohort groups, has their own set of shared concerns, expectations, and goals. Some groups develop around job functions or particular skill sets, around seniority level, or around a geographic location. These groups vary in numbers depending on the size and complexity of the business organization. Since the shared values of these groups can have a significant impact on the effectiveness of any company, development programs designed to address these values serve to the strengthen performance.

Newly hired employees are one such cohort group. They all require onboarding programs to transition into their roles in the company. Each new employee needs to learn about corporate culture; company policies and practices; operating and compliance procedures; personnel issues involving compensation, health benefits, vacation and sick time; and resources to continue their learning during and after the initial onboarding is completed.

Other cohort groups are more closely aligned by function and require programs that are more specialized. For instance, sales teams might benefit from programs related to prospecting for new clients; pitch and presentation tips; learning the parameters of profit margins and sales discounts; fulfillment and distribution mechanisms; and dealing with international clients or brokers. As employees who are both part of a cohort group (sales) but often work alone with clients, they might need additional specialized training regarding information management and internal communication.

High Potential. In every organization, there are groups of rising stars who are destined to become the next-level leaders in the company. Typically, they are identified by a demonstration of exceptional performance and are tracked as part of a leadership pipeline program. For these individuals, customized development is needed to prepare them for increased responsibility, particularly because most have exceeded expectations as individual contributors and promotion will entail the added responsibility of managing people.

A mid-market travel conglomerate in Miami identified high-potential managers and decided to enroll them in a three-week boot camp. The boot camp consisted of 35 hours of intensive classroom training on financial management and leadership essentials, five site visits to regional businesses to observe different management models, and one-to-one action learning projects focused on integrating lessons learned back in the workplace.

Executive education is another option that yields positive results for high-potential employees. Leading business schools around the world offer open-enrollment and customized programs for high-potential managers. These programs provide participants with insights on new research by the faculty and best-practice applications of that research in the field. Although programs can take place on site at the company, a significantly beneficial factor is taking employees away from work and its distractions, so that they can focus on the learning and on how to maximize their potential as new and emerging leaders.

Targeted. As new business needs and strategic priorities arise, specific development programs are needed to address them. After a merger or acquisition, for example, distinctly different cultures need to align and start working together with common policies. Cultural integration training that addresses practices, such as communication styles and processes, procedural norms, and strategy cascading, can subvert many alignment-related issues.

A financial services firm in Brisbane wanted to develop a social impact agenda. In particular, its objective was to teach the workforce and "friends and family" (investors, partners, and clients) about opportunities for community service, impact investing, and crowdsourcing sponsorship. Because much of this content was new to all involved, the CLO and leadership development group designed a series of modules to mirror the strategic objectives of the initiative.

Program development for affinity networks within companies is yet another focal area of targeted development. In an era when increasing diversity in the workplace and supporting diverse population groups is a growing priority, targeted development is certainly aligned with strategic objectives. Programs and initiatives developed for the general population do not always address special needs related to networks, such as gender, ethnicity, or ability.

A hospital in Indianapolis developed a program for male nurses focused on reacting to stereotypes, creating a comfortable environment and building a social cohort of support. Programs such as these can be targeted for particular priorities, demographic or affinity groups, or topic areas.

Client. A significant part of creating a learning organization and leveraging its resources can include offering development programs directly to clients. If designed and delivered correctly, these programs serve to facilitate communications between the company and the client, thereby increasing trust. These programs often are part of learning outreach initiatives. The free flow of information with clients strengthens relationships and leads to new business.

A management consulting firm in New York offers free training seminars to top clients twice a year. The day-long seminars focus on best practices related to topics including creating shareholder value, establishing trust in management, and building product innovation. Although this type of learning initiative does not directly or wholly satisfy learning objectives for the staff, it is a useful tool for enhancing the company-client partnership, and thus it directly fulfills a critical objective of the company.

Advisory Services

In addition to thought leadership initiatives and development programs, advisory services are the third pillar of the framework criteria for successful CILS. Advisory work is typically done one-on-one or in small groups and invokes more of a consultative methodology versus a teaching approach. This important component of the framework is particularly useful for gathering data, customizing individual design plans, and setting up ongoing implementation as learners face new challenges and situations that require support.

Assessment. In order to determine what skills or development a particular individual or team needs, a range of diagnostics are necessary. In larger companies with hundreds or thousands of employees, a formalized skills gap analysis serves to identify competencies needed by various segments of the organization and compares them to the existing assessment of where that individual or group currently stands. Learning managers work closely with their partners in Human Resources to implement assessment programs to address any gaps and find solutions.

Dan, a marketing manager in the consumer packaged goods industry in Camden, New Jersey, is responsible for building a new branding strategy for his product by leveraging social media and web 2.0 techniques. For 20 years, he had built B2C marketing solutions using more traditional channels (billboards, magazine placements, trade shows, and product promotions). Now, Dan needed to capitalize on his vast experience in the industry, while identifying the gaps in his knowledge that were needed for the new charge. Learning specialists from Dan's corporate university partnered with him to conduct this evaluation. After plotting his existing skill position and marking his aspirational position, Dan was then clear about the competencies he needed to develop to satisfy his new job responsibilities.

Resources are often not available to develop a full program of skill gap assessment and analysis in smaller companies. However, the need for assessment and staff advisory services are particularly important in small companies because their cost ratio of employee investment/retention to revenue is often greater. While resources for complex assessment tools might not be at their disposal, learning managers in these companies can achieve strong results by leveraging the close relationships that exist between managers and employees. By helping to create a corporate culture of openness and supportiveness in which employees feel free to seek advice about how best to achieve their goals, assessment becomes a natural part of the process. Individual employees can discuss their concerns and goals and the practical steps to take to address them.

Assessment tactics are also necessary for career development and succession planning. Increasingly, professional employees want to develop a long-term trajectory plan for their careers. What is the next job for them? What is the ultimate job for them? What is the path that will likely lead to their goals? How can planned learning initiatives help them with their plight? By going through a process similar to the one Dan followed, learning specialists can conduct quantitative and qualitative assessments to answer these questions and identify development opportunities that can guide and accelerate growth toward the dream job. Staff development advisory services is an effective method of retaining the best and brightest performers in the company.

Consulting. Practitioners in the office of the CLO are equipped to assist internal clients with planning and execution. Until recently, business managers and executives engaged outside firms to assist them with facilitation and planning needs. As the office of the CLO has developed into a more robust and comprehensive in-house development resource, more units are able to seek and receive support. Given the availability of the resource, managers should engage these practitioners for a variety of development needs. Team facilitation and planning is one example of a useful engagement.

Franc, a division manager in a retail bank in Montreal met with the CLO to discuss consulting for his team. His situation included:

1. Acculturating a new chief operating officer, a lateral hire from another bank, into his division
2. Restructuring the division to absorb the transition of temporary project consultants to full-time employees
3. A third quarter focus on 10 percent revenue growth
4. The integration of a new CRM reporting program

To address these, the CLO developed a proposal and recommendations for action and development. After selecting a plan, Franc then worked with the CLO office to implement it on a weekly basis, carefully paying attention to process, schedule, communication, and results.

For a company, providing value-added products and services to clients is the mission. Given the complexities of today's business environment and the increasing need to leverage learning and development to succeed, clients are finding consulting services in this area to also be a beneficial resource. The office of the CLO is equipped to provide a full range of learning services to customers and clients of the business. In larger companies, this office can supervise the creation of an actual division that offers consulting services to other companies to generate revenue. Once engaged, activities run the gamut from singular strategy discussion sessions to multi-incidence planning meetings to longitudinal project engagements. The value that the office of the CLO brings through consulting is in demand and therefore an internal and external differentiator.

ADP, the huge payroll management corporation with over half a million clients nationally, offers its clients consulting services. Its core business involves the design of payroll systems tailored to the needs of organizations large and small, the implementation of these systems, and ongoing customer support. In addition, the company has launched the Strategic Advisory Service, which consults with clients concerning the complicated area of benefits administration.

In smaller companies, external consulting for clients and vendors might be event or problem driven. Without the resources to dedicate the time and talent of internal experts to full-time consulting services, companies rely on seasoned professionals who have developed a longstanding relationship of trust and respect with their clients to provide this value-added benefit.

Coaching. In recent years, coaching has had the dual perception of being:

1. For staff who had a problem that needed "fixing" or required remedial focus
2. Facilitated by consultants who were external to the organization

Both are still partially true today. However, research shows that organizations are now using coaching more to positively support high performers and managers embarking on specialized assignments.

Executive and business coaches serve to clarify significant issues for individuals or teams who may be caught in routines that prevent their growth and effectiveness. It is instrumental in breaking through a functional "logjam" experienced by a manager or team. One of the most effective uses of coaching is to promote the professional growth of employees as they take on new responsibilities or ease into a new position.

Learning professionals in large organizations recruit staff members interested in training to be coaches. They create the training program internally or rely on outside coaching experts to design it. Smaller companies, without a dedicated corporate learning infrastructure, often rely on outside vendors to train staff inside to take on this function.

Josette is a partner in a tax accounting firm based in Hartford. She has been identified by her CEO and current board to be placed on a corporate board in another industry. The purpose is for her to gain experience with shareholder value as well as to establish visibility for her company in the investor marketplace. A coach was identified to assist Josette with this process by leveraging her network for exposure, constructing a concise narrative of value, identifying gaps in required contribution skills, and mapping potential industries and companies based on career goals. Individual executive coaching has significant value when used as a proactive supplement to aggressive growth and development goals.

Mentoring. Mentoring is another significant tool of advisory services that is supported in organizations large and small to develop and retain staff. It is an effective use of internal personnel resources with little or no dedicated cost to the company. Senior staff members are urged to engage in mentoring. In large organizations, it is often supervised by learning managers in cooperation with their partners in human resources. In smaller companies, mentoring is a function of the personal relationships that develop between seasoned employees or managers and less experienced staff members.

Peer mentoring is an effective component in the success of the development of new employees as well. In peer mentoring, established employees take on the responsibility of systematically supporting a colleague at the same level in the organization, but with less experience. In many cases, employees willing to take on this responsibility underscore their value to the company; it helps them as they proceed up the corporate ladder. Mentors meet regularly with their mentees to discuss any questions or problems concerning their jobs or the organization at large.

Mentoring at the executive level can be an effective adjunct to executive development programs. Reed became a managing director of a professional sports team in Dallas after serving 24 years as the chief operating officer of an executive search firm. As part of his onboarding process, the long-time general counsel of the executive team agreed to be his mentor. The mentorship lasted six weeks. They began by sharing information relative to understanding the professional sports industry and the team's profile and position therein. In their meetings, the mentor gave valuable advice about navigating the unique culture of the team to steer clear of pitfalls and traps by providing context through stories and anecdotes, as well as advice on a wide variety of operational issues. For Reed, the mentoring process, as a learning initiative, accelerated his transition by a year or more.

Summary

The foundation for a successful CILS program is setting up a framework for corporate learning inside and outside the organization. The framework enables the company to benefit from dynamic learning programs for the development of both employees and clients. The most effective way to construct this framework is through a three-pillar approach. These pillars are: Thought Leadership and Insight; Development Programs; and Advisory Services. Within the company, this learning framework enhances internal employee performance by developing the potential of employees and the teams in which they work. Outside the company, it strengthens client relations by providing direct value-added learning services and raising the profile of the company and its management in the industry as a prime source of information and advice.

CHAPTER 4

Understanding Barriers to Change

While executives often feel pressure to focus on shorter-term initiatives and priorities, devoting the time and resources to develop people is critically important and benefits the organization for the longer term.
—Joe DePinto, CEO, 7-Eleven, Dallas

If there is one constant about human behavior, it is resistance to change. We find this particularly true in business, particularly as we seek to understand the obstacles to the changes represented by implementing the Continuous Integration of Learning and Strategy (CILS) in an organization. Whether it is a multinational conglomerate or a corner store, there are two basic sets of obstacles: culture and cost (see Figure 4-1).

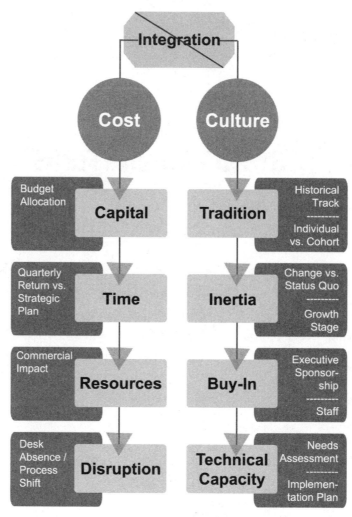

Figure 4-1 Barriers to Integrating Corporate Learning and Strategy

When a company decides to reorient itself into a true learning organization—one that has aligned business strategy and learning at every stage and constantly reassesses both in a mutually reinforcing loop of analysis and adjustment—there will be resistance from all of those who have a stake in, or rely on, the status quo. That is because CILS will change a much company's fundamental approach to the way it does business. Organizational and management structures will change. Reporting relationships will shift. The allocation of scarce resources will require greater scrutiny than ever. The processes of problem solving, strategic planning, and decision making will change.

Generally, these challenges to the status quo take the form of "gaps" in the stakeholders' understanding of how the changes will help make the company more vibrant and successful in comparison to existing business operations. In order for the dynamic integration of learning and corporate strategy to take hold, the learning team needs to acknowledge these gaps and find ways to close them.

The Culture Gap

Every company develops its own unique culture over time. This culture consists of a complicated mix of systems, attitudes, and values linked to the ways in which the organization accomplishes its goals. Culture pervades everything a business does and has a profound effect on how it grows and succeeds. It affects strategic decisions from hiring to product development to geographic expansion.

Corporate culture can be an asset to CILS. Successful companies have built their fortunes on the integrity of their unique cultures. The megatech companies of Google and Apple are famous for their cultures of innovation and inclusiveness. General Electric prides itself on its culture of preparation and competitiveness. Artisanal companies, from microbreweries to organic agribusinesses to manufacturers of fine furniture or clothing, consistently devote their resources to developing a culture of excellence—thereby promoting short- and long-term investments in human capital. Future chapters will discuss how CILS can be, and is supported by, a dynamic and influential culture of learning. But this chapter will look first at how any entrenched corporate culture can be an obstacle to the transformation of the business into a CILS-oriented learning organization.

Limited Tradition

Historical Absence. For many organizations, particularly those that are small or are/have been on an aggressive growth trajectory, the concept of a learning organization, or the presence of any formal development initiatives, is foreign. Although Chapter 1 comprehensively outlined how the "New Normals" changing landscape requires companies to develop and implement learning initiatives in order to survive, some thrived in the previous business context that was more regional, less technological, and slower to change. Further, others may have survived simply because of a unique differentiation in the marketplace that limited some of the typical competitive threats. As the environmental context changes, however, and the opportunities to succeed without a CILS model in place decrease, these companies are finding it particularly difficult to initiate change in their culture.

A culture that has been devoid of any learning and development activity has the most significant mindset shift to overcome. Leaders and staff alike have to absorb the burden of:

1. Building a case for change and enlightening key stakeholders
2. Establishing a base of infrastructure to support the development and operationalization of new efforts
3. Isolating, securing, or redirecting resources for the new purpose

Since many people in the organizations will never have seen or experienced any type of formal training event, not to mention one that was high-quality and best-in-class, the prospect of starting from scratch is a significant burden. Typically, the only path toward change is the small, incremental adoption of new initiatives. As success stories mount and impact examples begin to redefine a new cultural norm, change will be tolerated slowly, but likely not at the pace needed.

Misaligned Focus and Failed Attempts. For organizations that have a limited portfolio of development offerings, another reason for the failure to welcome change is not a lack of initiation, but a lack of success. Companies that have limited experience with corporate learning often create problems by launching a training event specifically as a form of innovation and change. That is, they do it just because it hasn't been done before, and they garner support and momentum based on the "new idea." In these cases, a needs assessment is rarely done, the timeline is typically rushed and too short, and the analysis and design protocol is misaligned. In other words, no one really knows what they are doing, but the opportunity to be unique and different, in support of an imminent business challenge, is attractive nonetheless.

An example includes an Armonk, New York, landscape management company that needed to quickly train its growing sales force on travel policies and protocols. For the majority of its history, staff rarely traveled. And, it was easy to manage and inform those who did. Now that the need for travel was increasing and more part-time contractors were participating, it seemed appropriate to formalize training requirements. The alternative was to continue to allow staff to learn travel requirements individually.

After deciding to custom develop an e-learning program, myriad problems ensued. First, since a thorough assessment of relevant data and needs had not been properly conducted, the new program was based on incomplete data. Protocols for managers wishing to travel internationally or via ferry, for example, were excluded. In addition, the administrative capability for making changes to the program as polices were adjusted was cumbersome and required, in some cases, a complete redesign—rendering the program useless almost from the beginning. Lastly, scope changes in the programming process escalated the cost to well over 75 percent of the budget.

The office of the CLO or its equivalent learning managers may feel pressured to design, develop, and offer a suite of new offerings before they are feasibly prepared to do so. This, in turn, leads to misaligned programs and, potentially, to a cultural backlash against offerings associated with the same or future strategic initiatives. In particular, stakeholders of organizational inertia or those insistent on maintaining the status quo gain strength for their arguments against CILS when it is not executed properly. They might present it as a "flavor-of-the-month" executive gameplay. Stakeholders for CILS can find themselves rushing to institute hastily constructed programs that put out fires rather than enrich the skill set of the company for the long term. This phenomenon pushes learning back to a position of "responsive training" rather than a proactive, strategic development.

Failed attempts at training initiatives not only hurt at the time of implementation, but also for months or years to come. Organizations are much less likely to initiate new plans and projects while failures loom in their recent institutional memory.

Individual Reward and Remediation. Another category of companies that have managed a limited portfolio of learning and development initiatives includes those that have targeted the highs and lows of individual employee performance. When formal training and development emerged with prominence in the 1950s, the primary focus was on rewarding successful individuals by teaching them the skills needed for the next level of responsibility. As discussed in Chapter 3, companies continue to use a wide range of techniques and efforts to reward stars—either as new joiners, high potentials, or recent promotes. The difficulty with this approach is that it is singular and tactical. CILS requires impact on the whole organization, thus this type of specialized focus is limiting.

On the other end of the spectrum, companies that use learning initiatives to "right-track" and support poor performers find this approach is also limiting. Any approach that singles out small populations of the total workforce will face the same barrier to change.

Organizational Inertia

Success Complacency. Catch phrases, such as "That's not how we do things here" or "If it ain't broke, don't fix it," indicate a resistance to embracing the changes CILS will inspire. This is true particularly if a business is reasonably successful. Nothing stands in the way of change more than continued success, even if it is a slowly declining success. As long as an organization can coast along, year to year, meeting modest goals, there is usually not an enormous amount of pressure to shake things up with learning initiatives.

In theory, a company needs to keep current in the marketplace and remain open to change to meet new demands. This is particularly true as business cycles tighten. But as long as things are going relatively well, there is a culture gap between inertia rooted in the status quo and the dynamism of progressive change through CILS. In their 2011 *Harvard Business Review* article, "Why Leaders Don't Learn from Success: Failures Get a Postmortem. Why Not Triumphs?," Harvard Business School professors Francesca Gino and Gary P. Pisano argue that businesses often do a good job of analyzing failures, but they can be less apt to evaluate the factors that have contributed to their success. They suggest that "the arrogance of success" breeds this analytical blind spot. Companies are inclined to investigate and dissect the details of failures with keen understanding. However, they do not apply the same analysis to what was responsible for their success and how they can continue to support it in the future. Success can become almost a dead end for some companies instead of a window into continued growth.

We have all seen the see the boilerplate investment caveat, "Past performance is no guarantee of future results," probably more times than we can count. We see it so often we probably stop registering it or taking it to heart.

Success can lead to complacency. Complacency, in turn, can lead to stagnation, and stagnation can lead to a loss of competitive edge, market share, then profitability. In other words, when at company is doing well, you need to work hard to do better because if you do not, somebody else will. Not to put too fine a point on it, success without the tools of progressive corporate learning contributes to the creation of one of the widest culture gaps.

Development Stages. Generally, the extent and character of the culture gap in relation to CILS is directly related to the corporation's stage of organizational evolution: first is start up; second is growth oriented; third is mature or established. At each stage of development, diverse factors contribute to the culture gap between maintaining business as usual and transformation to a learning organization.

Small start-up organizations are focused on almost everything at once—funding, hiring, product production or service development, branding, selling, keeping pace with the competition, and other priorities. But, more than anything else, they are obsessed with survival. New companies are founded for all kinds of reasons: the belief in an unmet demand for a product or service; the conviction that an existing product or service can be delivered better or more efficiently, or both; the notion that they are well positioned to offer a solution that meets a specialized or unique market need, and a host of others. But, until it can achieve some kind of consistent revenue and profit, its leadership drives forward putting out fires in crisis management mode. There is usually some basic planning with regard to systems, operations, and development—and theoretically, the more funding, the more planning—but still, there's a company-wide obsession with getting the job done however possible. Training is usually "on the job." Managers live in crisis mode. And, in almost all but the very best-funded cases, analysis, strategic planning, and reevaluation of internal systems takes a backseat to the challenges at hand.

In some ways, start-ups are the ultimate example of learning organizations. They are in a constant state of experimentation. If they do not learn their way to success, they are going to fail. This creates a culture of energy and openness, integrating ideas that work with strategic planning similar to an informal version of CILS. The dynamic new solutions the company finds by necessity can short circuit the path to an ongoing culture of learning. So long as they continue to serve their purpose and the company benefits, the culture gap between immediate practicality and CILS remains in place.

As organizations reach the second stage of development, their size and maturity requires a more structured approach. The culture gap between CILS and short-term success is likely to continue to widen. The number of employees grows. The layers of management expand. Corporate oversight, in the form of outside investors, directors, and shareholders, increases. The factors that contributed to first stage success take on the weight of routines. Routines have a way of becoming self-perpetuating systems and the foundation of a static corporate culture.

After a company has become established and profitable, the second-stage focus is often on growth and expansion. Access to greater resources through increased revenue and a general confidence in the future can obscure the need for self-evaluation and attention to progressive learning programs. When a company has "made it," there is a tendency to keep the momentum going doing business as usual. No need to rock the boat.

Some in the company may suggest that an analysis of the factors that contributed to its success is worthy of consideration. But for every voice that says, "Slow down, let's make sure we're laying the tracks correctly and maintaining them to keep the company moving in the right direction," there's a chorus of folks who accept market and competitive pressures to take advantage of momentum and surge forward, full-steam ahead. The culture gap between seizing the profits and investing in the future through CILS is broad.

As a company grows to maturity, its corporate structure becomes more complex. Multiple levels of management, satellite offices, and new strategic partnerships require an ever-expanding network of division-specific supervision. Often, as companies mature, the leadership implements a more systematic approach to their operations and, in so doing, creates a corporate culture bound by its own structure. The more complex the company, the harder it becomes to bridge the culture gap between the status quo and change through CILS.

Ironically, large and mature companies often employ many of the methodologies associated with corporate learning, such as data-driven planning, regular reporting on market forces, and long-range product development. They have the resources to commit to corporate learning initiatives and full implementation of CILS, but cannot proceed because of an entrenched corporate culture rooted in a "silo" mentality. ROI is the only "big picture" on management's screen. So long as each division contributes its share according to schedule, there is no need to tap into the synergistic potential that CILS has to offer.

If there is a culture gap between the status quo and change at each stage in a company's evolution, what does drive management to take steps to close it and accept CILS? Many companies do not recognize the need for a concerted CILS effort unless there is a problem that raises the possibility of declines in market share, revenue, profit, and investor return. The threat of these bad outcomes may push senior leaders to consider implementing learning programs that they have either ignored or rejected in the past. However, it requires serious and sustained commitment from the top to overcome the culture of habit and inertia. Even under these conditions, key stakeholders are likely to resist the implementation of learning initiatives as "soft" solutions and push back against the integration of learning and strategy as a distraction from the "real problems at hand."

Executive Buy-In

Culture starts at the top. The C-suite sets the tone and tenor of a corporation's internal culture. Look at as Google's commitment to innovation and creativity that grew out of founders Larry Page's and Sergey Brin's work together at Stanford, or the dedication to customer service and ease of execution promoted by CEO Jeff Bezos at Amazon. The culture of just about every company has its roots in the vision of its founders and their successors. To overcome the internal resistance to transforming a business into an integrated learning organization through CILS requires strong buy-in at the top. The trouble is that this form of internal resistance is often strongest at that level.

Experience and Influence. Most senior executives today have not benefited from the opportunity to work, at any point in their career, for an organization that leveraged a CILS-type model. This is largely due to the fact that comprehensive learning organizations are a relatively new phenomenon and most executives achieved their positions before the significant increase in adoption of such programs that have occurred over the last 15 years.

As a result of this lack of experience, executives are typically skeptical about claims that a CILS approach is necessary for real business success. Since they have been extremely successful using a CILS-less approach, convincing them otherwise is a tall order. The argument about the need to adjust to the threat of a new and changing landscape is one that they've heard before—and they have overcome those threats in the past. The difference is that the innovations in strategy that worked during those earlier episodes are no longer as relevant. CILS is the answer for today's strategic adjustment, but convincing them that this is now *the* answer poses a real challenge.

Given the lack of exposure that CEOs and top executives have had with learning and development, it is incumbent on the CLO (or designated executive) to provide advice and counsel on strategic approaches. If the role does not exist, or if it doesn't have the necessary access or influence, then obtaining executive buy-in to implement CILS will encounter a significant barrier.

Profit-and-Loss (P&L) Dilemma. Just as there is a culture gap between the status quo and the commitment to change, there is a leadership gap between a profit-driven focus on ROI and a visionary approach to future growth and profitability. CEOs and other senior managers often view their roles as the keepers of the corporate flame. They need to keep it burning as brightly as possible. In today's market, that means delivering an ever-higher short-term ROI. In the race against accelerated market cycles and spiraling costs, corporate leaders often see learning initiatives as long-term investments, which yield less tangible contributions to the bottom line.

In his book, *Managerial Leadership*, Peter Topping writes that not knowing what may happen in the future often leads to heightened anxiety in the present. Resistance to change is a successful anxiety-reducing action. This idea is particularly prevalent in top corporate leadership. While their role in the organization is to plan for future growth, leaders often base their strategic decisions on existing models that have worked in the past rather than on new approaches in an effort to get the job done. CILS is a forward-thinking process. It takes time and resources—both of which many corporate leaders deem scarce commodities that need to be applied elsewhere.

In response to market research that indicated the growing need for organic pet products, the CEO of a pet food manufacturer in Des Moines proposed launching an all-organic line of products for its retail household market. The challenge was to produce and market this new line to customers without cannibalizing resources for the existing product lines. Because the company had no prior experience with organic products, a significant learning initiative was required to educate employees about this new corporate initiative. All the existing departments needed an immersion course in organic pet food, from sourcing to production to marketing and distribution. The competition was gaining ground quickly, and there was market pressure to launch and promote the new product line as soon as possible.

The CEO wanted to overcome the learning gap by hiring a dedicated "SWAT team" of individuals with specific experience in organic pet food. However, this approach was costly, adding to the fixed overhead, and would not close the learning gap in the existing staff. The office of the CLO recommended a different approach. After a cost-benefit analysis determined that adding highly paid "experts" in the form of an entirely new team of employees would erode rather than add to the investment in this new venture and push back its profitability to an unacceptable level, it proposed a targeted learning and development plan for a subset of the in-house teams. This analysis suggested in-house training by expert consultants in the field would be faster and less expensive than hiring a new team and would have greater long-term positive impact on the company as a whole.

The CEO would not budge. Focused only on the short-term goal of bringing a new product to market as quickly as possible, she did not recognize the value of an integrated training and product development process. She just wanted to "get the job done." In the end, they reached a compromise by hiring an outside manager for the new division with experience in the field who worked directly with the learning professionals to train existing staff and get the campaign off the ground as quickly as possible. But overcoming the corporate impasse cost the company valuable time that could have been leveraged to combat the competition. If senior leadership had taken a stronger position in support of the CLO, the gap in leadership priorities between short-term and long-term could have been resolved more quickly to the company's overall benefit.

As the Chief Development Officer of an international not-for-profit based in Washington, D.C., Joe supervised a wide variety of programs dealing with adult educational access, healthcare, and wellness issues. The organization secured a long-term, recurring funding commitment from a group of new donors—but it came with a condition. The donors wanted the strategic focus of the programming group to expand to include a "Children and Youth" portfolio in addition to the existing adult-oriented portfolios. Given that Joe's entire 25-year career had been focused on research and programming related to adults, this new directive presented a significant challenge to him personally.

At first, he resisted the program, arguing that it was outside the organization's mandate and that it would require a substantial shift in resources. His team was not prepared for this new set of goals, and it would take time for bring them up to speed. Joe was committed to challenge the new direction and, in doing so, he created a leadership gap. However, the director of the group was adamant about gaining access to the new funding because it would benefit the long-term goals of the organization. In this case, senior management supported whatever changes were necessary to close the leadership gap and get on with the new set of priorities.

Realizing that his directive was clear, Joe went into action. Working with his learning professionals, he commissioned a market analysis of existing programs targeting young people. Armed with this data, he and his team proposed a series of development programs that suited the overall goals of his organization and the new donors. Once approved, he worked with a combination of internal and external consultants to design and implement the programs.

Staff Buy-In

The collective resistance to change manifests on the individual employee level as well. As changes in learning and development are introduced, staff concerns include whether the necessary time and commitment is worth the effort, whether their managers truly support their participation, and whether their skills and capabilities are no longer appreciated as being adequate.

Cost-Benefit Understanding. Learning and development initiatives require a significant amount of investment. No investment is greater than that of the employees or participants themselves. Because of the high level of commitment that is required, resistance is often pretty strong. First of all, training takes time: If conducted during the work day, arrangements to make up missed time will be required. If conducted after work, a strong justification for infringing on personal time will be necessary.

Participation also takes a high level of engagement. Actively participating in sessions, studying follow-up materials, contributing to group projects, and preparing for evaluation components all require a high level of focus.

In many cases, participating in learning initiatives also requires sponsorship from senior managers. Given that precious political capital may need to be expended, concerned comments may include:

"How important is participating, really? Will it be worth it?"

117

"If my manager is not fully supportive, am I jeopardizing
my relationship or job?"

Remembering that the priority for most employees is to
do their jobs well and keep their jobs, helping them understand how training initiatives can function in support
of those objectives is key to beginning a process of overall
cultural change.

Skills Threat and Trust. If a corporation is not a learning
organization, the values represented by CILS initiatives
might threaten staff members' sense of security, which
results in a barrier gap. All change is accompanied by
uncertainty, and uncertainty is usually uncomfortable, especially in the business environment. Learning-related
change, with its implication that existing skills and knowledge will no longer be sufficient to achieve the goals of
the organization, can compound the high-level resistance
in management.

Trust and transparency are extremely important to
overcoming resistance to learning initiatives and CILS
implementation. John Kotter in his book, *What Leaders
Do*, highlights the importance of these factors as vital to
the success of any organization dedicated to becoming a
learning organization. Employees are much less likely to
resist a CILS plan when they understand the rationale behind it, the way it will work, what it will mean for them,
and the new opportunities it can create. And the converse,
of course, is true. When employees believe that changes

will have a negative effect on their workloads, compensation, or careers, they are much more likely to resist.

Company-wide learning initiatives play a powerful role in combating the employee gap. Clear and pragmatic communication of the organization's priority is the first step to creating an atmosphere of trust and community. Every staff member needs to buy-in to the culture of learning by understanding how it will work. Without this basic step, any shift in corporate priority will be met with resistance and take longer to implement.

An example of the importance of internal communication in facilitating change is the situation regarding emergency room (ER) technicians in a hospital in Brussels. The hospital had instituted a series of wage cuts, layoffs, and reorganizations. Management did not handle these necessary changes in a clear and honest way, often not offering any explanation or seeking input from the people who would be affected. When management briefed this highly skilled group about plans to install new machines that would dispense medications in place of full-service pharmacies, employees were skeptical that it was just another ploy to cut staff and increase the workload. The present system had been working well for decades. Why change it? The answer from management was that this change would help them better serve the patients. The ER technicians had heard this catchphrase before and did not believe it.

In addition, the ER technicians would be required to participate in intensive training to learn the use of these and other robotic devices planned for the hospital. This alone would add to their workload. Their continued resistance to the new programs delayed full participation in the training program, and this delay had a significant and negative impact on the deployment of the dispensing machines. Eventually, the new system was put in place, but not without continued mistrust of management by staff members. The lesson here is that management should have addressed trust issues in the workplace before charging ahead with this new initiative. Management needed to build trust by communicating the reasoning behind the change and working to get the technicians' buy-in to facilitate the process.

When employees resist the implementation of CILS, it requires unified leadership at the top of the organizational pyramid to communicate the nature and value of the proposed changes. This is the one of the principal characteristics of a learning organization. Clear communication of the company's goals and their implementation through corporate learning are the best ways to overcome the employee gap.

The Cost Gap

The twin pressures of global competition and the incessant emphasis on short-term returns have made it harder than ever to find resources for long-term investment in CILS. While CILS will ultimately help a company to overcome its financial performance challenges better and more efficiently, it becomes caught in the resource gap when compared to funding options that can yield bottom line results faster. This gap represents a gulf in allocation priorities between projects deemed necessary to yield results in the short term and those that might be important for the future, but not immediately necessary for the survival of the organization.

Budget Priorities

The allocation of resources, or operating funds, is the first priority in the budgeting process of any business. Physical facilities, technology upgrades, marketing and investment plans, salaries and benefit packages, hiring new talent, research and development, and general overhead costs are among the concrete and easily quantifiable areas that require annual investment to keep the company functioning.

Short-Term versus Long-Term Investments. Because business is about the bottom line, the challenge in bridging the resource gap involves accepting the role of CILS in the financial health and growth of the organization. As CILS is a relatively new form of long-term investment, it effectively faces serial budget hurdles. First, it must pass the test that all long-term investments face. Given all the pressing demands for short-term results, is it a worthwhile expenditure? Once it clears that hurdle, CILS must compete against all the other, more widely accepted long-term expenditures that produce tangible contributions to revenue.

Again, the budgeting process offers internal stakeholders who are against CILS a huge advantage. They can pay lip service to the *idea* of integrated learning with strategic planning while lobbying against the funding necessary to turn it into a reality.

The CEO of a multinational pulp and paper manufacturer based in Santiago kept receiving reports that the high fees charged by their outsourced trucking companies were not warranted by the level of service they delivered. As a result, the CEO proposed that they eliminate these outside vendors, take on the delivery of materials using company-leased or purchased trucks, and train in-house staff to drive and maintain the vehicles. While this called for a much higher fixed cost investment in the short term, the CEO argued that it would give the company more control over its distribution, allow it to provide better service to its customers, and contribute to a more reliable revenue stream in the future. The CLO pointed out that the projected costs of this new venture did not include the cost of the training programs, additional supervisory personnel necessary to implement this new program, operational and safety hazards, related insurance and risk liabilities, and storage, security, and repair needs. The learning team suggested they do a full analysis of the costs before making a decision, taking into consideration the ongoing CILS programs needed.

However, plagued by delays and customer complaints, the CEO argued against further analysis. The company could not afford to wait any longer to fix this problem.

The board of directors agreed and decided against the additional CILS expenditure for analysis. Once implemented, the unforeseen costs of the new program skyrocketed. Lack of coordinated training programs resulted in a series of delays that set back the operation and garnered additional customer complaints. Poor storage facilities and incompetent maintenance of the trucks, coupled with driving accidents and the consequent increase in insurance costs, crippled the program. The CEO authorized additional resources to institute CILS programs to find solutions to these operational problems. Eventually, the entire project was revamped into a combination of internal and outsourced vehicles and personnel.

Quantification and Commercial Impact. The benefits of CILS and learning initiatives, while vital to the future of any organization, are difficult to quantify in return-on-investment dollars. The time and talent of staff are speculative assets without the kind of objective value found in more concrete corporate assets, such as infrastructure or marketing efforts. Yet, without the concerted efforts of the its staff, no company can thrive and achieve any of its goals.

Learning initiatives also carry an unwanted stigma of not being commercially additive. In businesses, functions that directly generate revenue are heralded as the most valuable—product development and sales, for example. Revenue-support functions that are very closely aligned to those primary functions are next in line—marketing and business development, for example. But, if learning initiatives are classified and perceived strictly as a revenue-support function, instead of one that is core to strategic operations, its contribution to the commercial success of the company will be minimized or dismissed.

CILS evaluates and sharpens these efforts so that each and every person associated with the organization works at his or her full potential. Recognition of the integral role of CILS plays in achieving a successful ROI by decision makers and financial planners can lessen the resource gap.

Disruption of Routine

In addition to serving as a cultural barrier, timing may also serve as an indirect cost barrier. The unpredictability of work events may unintentionally overlap with training time and cause gaps in productivity that ultimately cost the company money.

Although it has been established that learning initiatives ultimately contribute positively to the company's bottom line, any time spent away from work is often seen as a counteracting cost activity. If time is money and people make money for the company while at work, then any time away from work is effectively costing the company money. Scheduled programming can usually avert any conflict, but surprise events in the work environment are often hard to predict.

For example, if a client meeting is scheduled at the last minute—and at the same time as a preplanned learning initiative, there is an unfortunate dilemma. If the employee chooses to attend the training for which funding was already allocated and the client relationship is negatively affected as a result, concerns about future participation will be apparent. The eventual benefits of the activity create a circular conversation where any losses are realized in time. However, the short-term sacrifice is a cost barrier that continues to prevent some organizations from changing.

Overall, bridging the cost gap requires that management put CILS on par with all other prioritized corporate investments. All funding decisions concerning CILS fall into two broad categories:

1. Those related to long-term plans with clear deliverables
2. Just-in-time programs that respond to unplanned events and short-term challenges or opportunities

Both sets of investments require dedicated line-items in the budget for long-term initiatives as part of the overall strategic business plan and funding for special projects that cannot be predicted.

Summary

The four barriers to CILS implementation manifest themselves as "gaps" between the changes learning initiatives make to an organization and the company's commitment to business as usual. Resistance to the changes that accompany a commitment to CILS can come from all quarters in an organization. The culture gap is the struggle between maintaining the status quo in an organization and the need for change. The leadership gap is the conflict between management's pressure to balance short-term goals for ROI with its long-term investment in growth and development. The employee gap involves overcoming the skepticism of staff regarding the impact of learning initiatives on their roles in the organization. Finally, there is the resource gap, in which investment in a CILS initiative must compete for funding dollars against concrete, quantifiable expenditures.

Regardless of the size or growth stage of a company, its leaders and staff members need to support CILS if it is to succeed. Short-sighted planning that subverts the long-term benefits of corporate learning and CILS comprise the greatest barrier to its acceptance.

CHAPTER 5

ROL: Return on Learning

Companies that pride themselves in their superior commitment to customers and clients must show parallel dedication to their own people. This is the only way to realize the maximum investment.
—Eric Foss, President and CEO, Aramark, Philadelphia

The primary goal of the Continuous Integration of Learning and Strategy (CILS) is to give an organization the tools it needs to achieve its strategic goals, succeed, and thrive. To be effective, CILS requires an ongoing commitment to allocating resources to keep the effort functioning at full capacity. While the benefits of being a learning organization are clear in theory, in practice such organizations are often scrutinized and criticized as not yielding identifiable contributions to the bottom line. As discussed in Chapter 4, there is often a cost barrier associated with CILS initiatives. In the resource-scarce, return-focused world in which every business operates today, the senior leadership in organizations needs to ask the same question of corporate learning programs as it does of other expenditures: Is the return on investment (ROI) apparent and justified? What are the best ways to quantify the Return on Learning (ROL) in financial terms?

Measuring the return on learning investments is more difficult than measuring the return on other, more tangible, investments. If a company spends money on R&D and produces a new product, then successfully test markets it and sells it profitably, the ROI is easily attributable. If a company invests in a major software upgrade to its call center management system, it is relatively easy to compare money out (the cost of the upgrade) and money in (increased revenue through the ability to process more sales calls more efficiently) to evaluate its ROI.

However, the ROL of CILS initiatives are a bit more difficult to quantify. One reason is that in any learning organization, the CILS initiative influences nearly every aspect of the operation. From strategic planning to data accumulation and analysis, from operational systems management to facility expansion, from ongoing training of staff to in-reach and outreach communications and a host of other aspects of a fully functioning organization, the CILS process and associated team affects the organization as a whole, as well as many of its individual divisions. Unlike many specific expenditures, which tend to be distinct

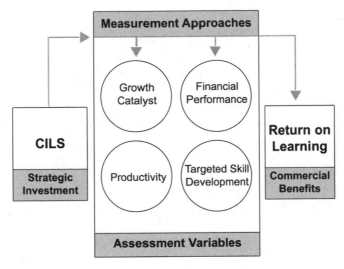

Figure 5-1 CILS Return Formula

and finite by nature, CILS is a moving target in terms of evaluation simply because it has so many facets and members (see Figure 5-1).

Measurement Approaches

How can management measure ROL? Two fundamental metric approaches help to understand the financial impact CILS has on the bottom line: the macro and the micro approaches.

Macro

In the macro approach, management measures the overall success of the entire organization in achieving its financial goals. Putting aside unforeseen market forces and economic upheavals, a learning organization that meets the financial milestones set by its CEO and board of directors owes a strong portion of that success to its support of a dynamic CILS company-wide program. With its continuous oversight of the effectiveness on internal systems, regular analysis of data and reports, staff training and special targeted programs, CILS provides a pathway to the success of nearly every division of the company. The ROI of the entire organization means that the ROL of CILS is strong as well.

However, this "big picture" approach will require some historical perspective. To measure the overall ROL, the financial team needs to look at the ROI of the organization several years before it made the transition to a leaning organization and instituted CILS. Corporate annual reports for several years before the transition should yield the data required. Then, the financial team should compare these to the reports from the first two years after the introduction of CILS to get a sense of how the transition affected the overall ROI. Finally, the most current financial performance report, created after CILS had been up and running, will offer a snapshot of the present ROI of the company. Factoring in such variables as inflation and changes in the economy, this historical research should give management a quantified accounting of ROL.

Micro

The micro approach evaluates the ROL of specific CILS programs designed to achieve strategic goals. Once the CEO approves the expenditure for the particular learning program, the financial team can monitor its success on a cost/benefit basis. As described in Chapter 2, the office of the CLO should establish mechanisms for evaluating such programs to continue to validate efficacy and improve them through subsequent revisions and iterations. A successful outcome invariably indicates a strong ROL. Again, key quantitative metric variables include:

- Attendance and participation rates
- Assessment and exam scores
- Performance reviews scores (i.e., manager and peer feedback)
- Individual job improvement proficiencies (i.e., decreased time to reach sales quota)
- Job promotion rates
- Individual job retention rates (i.e., decreased attrition)

Key qualitative metrics include:

- Mentoring, leadership, and skill transfer cascading
- Job satisfaction levels
- Client satisfaction levels
- Cultural motivation
- Product and process innovation

Where the macro approach seeks to determine if the integration of learning and strategy, as a planned tactic, stimulates enhanced returns, the micro approach isolates the CILS contribution as a piece of the solution and measures its direct impact on ROL.

Key Variables

Both approaches to quantify ROL require that an organization view the results on several levels. There is the ultimate level of the macro approach, which analyzes the contribution CILS made to the bottom line ROI of the organization. Then, there is the micro approach, which ascertains the impact of CILS on the success of particular programs in addressing the company's strategic goals. There are also methods to assess the ROL as it affects areas of the operation that are less definable, but are significant to the success of the organization.

External Network. One such area is the relationship between clients, vendors, and outside partners on the one hand and the company on the other. Analysis of the impact of CILS programs on this area comprises the "outside-in" perspective. Are clients happier after the changes made to company through CILS? Are they more likely to continue and grow their business with the company? Are they more likely to vouch for the company to other potential clients? Have the learning programs made relations with clients and vendors more transparent, efficient, and beneficial? Has the confidence level of outside financial partners, such as investors, shareholders and financial institutions, in the company's ability to set and meet its strategic goals and meet its growth targets become stronger? The answers to these questions offer some perspective on the overall efficacy of the learning programs.

Part of what it means to be a learning organization includes keeping in touch with this wide network of professional affiliates and understanding their attitudes regarding the company and its future. Gaining perspective on the organization through the eyes of its outside partners gives management a strong sense of the ROLs an organization has achieved. Formal and informal client surveys are one way to gather this information. Regular "check-ins" with key personnel on the front line of client and investor relations is another way gain insights into the company's industry profile.

Internal Network. The "inside-out" perspective is important to get a "nuts-and-bolts" sense of how well CILS is working internally. The overarching goal of corporate learning is *organizational* improvement. One of the most dramatic indicators of ROL is the benefits derived from these programs by the staff. To gain this perspective, it is important to assess the performance of the group of employees who participated in the learning programs. Do the managers and other corporate leaders with responsibility for achieving the strategic goals linked to a given learning initiative find measurable benefits from the initiative?

Did the participants actually gain the progressive skills the program promised to teach? How did their participation affect their morale? What affect does ongoing participation have on retention, promotion, and individual growth?

Once again, both formal and informal periodic surveys will yield this information. Focus groups or even town hall meetings with company management are effective methods to get qualitative feedback from participants and other employees that can be used to inform and improve future initiatives. In more technical areas, employees might be asked to take skills tests in order to measure whether or not the intended skills were learned and how well.

The principal character of any learning organization is self-analysis. Taking the pulse of the organization on continuous basis is key to the evaluation of the ROL. Reactions and results change over time, and an accurate assessment of the value of any learning initiative has to measure those changes.

On an organizational level, of course, basic performance metrics are a critical factor—perhaps the most critical— of assessing the ROL. But comprehensive assessment of learning initiatives should employ a broad range of tools that are applied in direct relation to the subject of and the question behind a given assessment. And, tracking the long-term satisfaction and success of learning participants—and all employees, for that matter—will provide additional evidence of the organizational return, or lack thereof, of CILS across the board.

Whatever the approach taken to gain some perspective on corporate learning, there are four metrics to measure the ROL. They are financial performance, productivity, targeted skill development (TSD), and growth catalyst. The application of these metrics to the overall organization's performance or the success of a particular initiative forms the basis for assessing the ROL and the attendant ROI of CILS.

Financial Performance

Setting financial performance goals is the primary and most straightforward driver of any company's strategic plan. Basically, it is a simple equation: approved investments need to achieve a projected level of financial return. As a result of today's accelerated business cycles, management sets an annual goal for financial performance for the entire corporation, but evaluates performance on a quarterly basis. Specific plans for investments approved to achieve specific goals undergo scrutiny on a rolling basis. In learning organizations, CILS programs are instrumental in all stages of the planning, implementation, and evaluation of financial performance, including its own.

A company based in Paris makes a line of specialty cosmetics. In its first three years of operations, the company sold its products exclusively through a team of sales representatives with responsibility for specific geographic territories. The reps made in-person calls to large department store buyers and the owners or managers of local boutiques alike. This traditional method was costly and cumbersome, but always met its goals. Unlike its competitors, the company did not invest in an online direct-to-commercial presence. The growing success of the company made it a target for takeover by a large international manufacturer of beauty products. However, the larger company had a successful online portal and full customer care division. In order to meet the aggressive financial performance goals set by the new parent organization, the senior management of the specialty company needed to integrate its sales operation to interface successfully with the new parent company's ecommerce and customer service divisions.

In response to this strategic goal, the learning professionals in both companies worked together to create a series of programs to facilitate this integration. These programs involved new information systems, inventory and distribution controls, sales training, reorganization, and streamlining of the sales force. The investment in these learning programs paid off. Once the implementation of the new systems was fully functioning, the additional revenue stream of ecommerce helped the specialty company achieve the parent company's financial performance goals. Commercial retail buyers could address any fulfillment issues they had with the customer service instead of relying on sales reps as before. The ROL of these CILS efforts clearly contributed to the overall ROI of the organization.

The ROL investments designed to produce cost savings is an important aspect of financial performance. Efficiency cuts waste and strengthens the bottom line. The analytical tools of CILS position it uniquely to pinpoint ways to save resources.

The CEO of a manufacturer of prefabricated housing in Scranton, Pennsylvania, noticed a slow but steady decline in the company's profit margin. On analysis by the CLO and learning team, the cause became apparent. They were the result of the inefficiencies of a decentralized production system. His company, which was formed by a series of acquisitions of smaller companies throughout the Midwest, operated eight different plants. Each of the plants operated semiautonomously, with each handling its own procurement, supplier management, and fulfillment. As the company grew, this decentralized system became inefficient and wasted resources through replication and inconsistent pricing.

Tasked with addressing the changes necessary to cut waste, the learning team proposed a new system to take advantage of the combined buying power of all eight plants through a centralized procurement process. The learning professionals designed the plan of realignment of resources by creating a new procurement division that worked closely with the supply needs of each factory. Once implemented, the cost of goods decreased substantially and profitability began to increase to meet approved financial performance goals. The ROL of these learning initiatives went right to the overall ROI of the organization.

Productivity

Productivity is the lifeblood of any organization and is inextricably linked to financial performance. The more goods and services a company produces to meet demand, the more revenue it takes in. Like financial performance, CILS programs have a direct impact on the higher and more efficient productivity in any learning corporation.

Take the example of a cellular company based in Kansas City, Missouri, seeking to upgrade its customer care call centers. For years, its call centers relied on banks of live operators. Each operator was responsible for speaking directly to customers, asking a few questions to identify the nature of the call, and then they either taking the order or trying to solve the customer complaint. In the fast-paced world of direct-to-consumer commerce, this system was too slow. While it created an outside profile of the company caring about personal customer care, this system created numerous delays based on the volume and nature of calls at any given time. Sometimes, the operators had more incoming calls then they could handle, creating a bottleneck that left customers on hold or subjected them to the frustration of endless ringing. Customers began to look to its competitors for quicker service. Revenue started to decline.

The CEO rallied support for the replacement of the existing system with a software-driven call management system. The proposal had been previously raised at several annual meetings, but the CFO and VP of Sales successfully challenged the initiative, citing the high upfront purchase cost and the challenge of transitioning the support techs to use such a system. However, in the face of growing pressure from competitors using digital systems, the CEO commissioned a cost-benefit analysis of the project. The report demonstrated that the purchase and installation of the new automated call management system would pay for itself based on increased capacity to deal with a higher volume of calls, a reduction in staff, and greater customer satisfaction.

Presented with the potential impact of the new system on productivity, senior management approved the program. While the initial investment in the new system and in-house staff training was steep, the subsequent increased revenue and per-call efficiencies resulted in a substantial return to profitability. The new call management system reduced customer frustration by eliminating the operator bottleneck and ensuring that every call was answered by the second ring. As a result, increased productivity led to an increase in revenue that exceeded projections. The ROL demonstrated by the increased productivity resulting from the CILS analysis and implementation of the new system was clear.

The range of possibilities related to increased productivity through learning programs is virtually limitless in today's technological environment. CILS professionals regularly analyze productivity systems, compare them to competitors, and search for ways to improve them by borrowing ideas, developing new ones, or both. The ROI from learning programs that serve to reduce manufacturing costs, increase time-to-market efficiency, and streamline supply and distribution help to quantify ROL without difficulty.

Targeted Skill Development (TSD)

Depending on the strategic imperative, the effectiveness of CILS on the progressive improvement of staff and its overall impact on the corporate bottom line is another metric used to measure ROL. When a challenge arises, a company must decide whether to educate existing personnel, outsource consultants, or hire and train new employees. To determine which option is best, learning professionals assess the cost-benefit of each and propose the most appropriate method to best achieve the company's goal. Once the decision is made and the program installed, learning professionals follow up with a detailed assessment of its success and resulting ROL for the company.

Targeted skill development is one of the most important functions of learning initiatives. The progressive development of staff yields all kinds of benefits to the organization. Employees deepen their specific skill sets and are more effective in executing their jobs. Coaching, mentoring, and training helps develop future managers. Effective sourcing of executives and in-house experts decreases the company's reliance on outside consultants. At the end of the day, TSD is a strong metric in evaluating ROL.

A beverage company in Hartford established a strategic goal of expanding to the emerging market in the Middle East. It has engaged in international, emerging market expansion before, with excellent results in Eastern Europe. Corporate leadership wanted to use the same team that led the expansion into Eastern Europe to lead the expansion into the Middle East. However, none of the European team members have ever worked in the Middle East and needed training in order to familiarize themselves with the regulatory and compliance schemes of the target markets there. In addition, they needed to be educated to gain insight into local customs and cultural preferences that will help shape their marketing efforts.

The CILS team analyzed the challenges to this strategic goal, which included language and cultural diversities in the large region, distribution, and marketing efforts, such as point of purchase displays, advertising, and promotion. While the team's report determined that the European team lacked the personnel and experiences to meet this strategic challenge, there were members of the international marketing division who had experience living and working in the Middle Eastern region. The CILS recommended a suite of TSD programs to train these staff members to manage the effort, with substantial support from the European team.

In this example, some of the costs associated with the CILS analysis and recommendations are relatively easy to measure. For instance, how much did it cost to train the expansion team and "build" the knowledge base internally? What were the costs of hiring and training new staff to take the place of the members of the new team? Other effects, however, are harder to measure, such as the time and talent drain from the European team to help train the new staff. Was there a significant impact on the morale of the European team when the decision was made to take them off the project? The best indication of the ROL in this situation was the ultimate success in achieving a substantial market share in the Middle East in line with budget projections.

Another way to evaluate the ROL using TSD is determining how successful it has been in helping diverse groups of employees work together more effectively. For example, a software start-up launched a next generation messaging app. To increase the security of its messaging platform, its leadership agreed to merge with a well-established encryption company. The average age of the engineers at the start-up was only 23, while the average age of the engineers at the encryption company was nearly 40. This created an unanticipated culture gap between the two sets of engineers, which interfered with the integration of the units. Each unit had age-linked differences in approaches to time management, collaboration, strategic goals, and work habits. It became apparent that the two engineering teams were having difficulty working together. As a result, productivity suffered. The learning professional in the encryption company proposed a three-day offsite workshop designed to address the culture gap by encouraging a focus on shared interests, goals, and commitment to results. After the session, there was a notable improvement in cooperation and morale that led to increased productivity. The investment in the logistics of the workshop, a concrete cost, and the lost time in the office of key staff members, a less concrete cost, paid off. The effort integrated both teams into one engineering department and facilitated the design of secure, new products.

Growth Catalyst

One of the fundamental goals of any corporation is growth. CILS performs a vital function as a catalyst to achieve this goal. In particular, learning programs are effective in helping companies plan and manage the steps necessary for profitable growth. Some of the areas targeted are new product development, expansion through acquisitions, and building on existing facilities and staff. Again, the success of the growth initiative is directly linked to the role CILS plays in it. The ROL of the programs responsible for the achievement of this strategic goal can then be measured in terms of profitability.

New owners purchased a mid-size candy confectioner in Vermont to manufacture candy for the holiday market. As with many businesses that service retailers during the holidays, the traditional cycle of their business was boom or bust. According to the National Retail Federation, holiday sales represent nearly 20 percent of all sales in the United States—and for some retailers that percentage climbs to as high as 40 percent. During preparations for the peak holiday seasons, the company's factory ran on overtime to meet the surge in demand. It hired temporary workers to help keep the flow of product coming and added to its distribution division by subcontracting deliveries to several outside companies. Then, once the clients received their products, the revenue stream fell off precipitously. Many of the good workers the company had hired and trained were let go. The factory functioned at less than half capacity.

The management set a strategic goal for the upcoming year to stabilize revenue and increase permanent growth. How could the company derive permanent growth from this yo-yo business model? Working with sales, marketing, and manufacturing, the learning professionals of the company did a market analysis. Their report found that many of clients had a need for unique, nonseasonal candy throughout the year. They reported that with some additional investment in developing new products, expanding the facility, and additional training of staff, the company could create a new division to service this ongoing need between peak seasons. A cost/benefit analysis projected an increase in the ROI after the first six months of operation. The CEO approved the plan.

The transition was rocky at first. Research into new kinds of nonholiday candy was tough, especially given the competition. Branding efforts of the new candy lines was a challenge and the new equipment required more adjustment than originally planned, but the new division was up and running only slightly behind schedule. CILS employed targeted skill development programs to select, train, and retain the best seasonal workers for the new effort. Eventually, demand for the new products grew strong enough to run the new equipment during the peak holiday seasons as well. The new division met the goals for the ROI. The success of the new division underscored the ROL.

Summary

Businesses make investments expecting to see high returns. CILS represents a fundamental investment of money, time, and talent in the future of the company. Just as with any other corporate expenditure, CILS initiatives need to demonstrate an ROL. There are a variety of methods available to management to evaluate ROL. Successful analysis on a macro level of the general profitability of the company as a whole is one approach. Another is to evaluate the ROL of CILS on a micro level by assessing the cost-benefit of programs designed to achieve strategic goals. Perspectives on the ROL both from inside and outside of the organization can yield additional insights.

The four key areas that learning advocates and corporate leaders use to assess ROL are: financial performance, productivity, targeted skill development, and growth catalyst. Each of these areas is basic to the success of CILS in any learning organization.

As much as quantifying ROL is a prerequisite to the continued funding of learning efforts, it is also worth remembering that constant, ongoing assessment of the efficacy of learning initiatives is at the core of CILS. Learning organizations engage in the continuous evaluation of performance, innovation, and improvement. Quantifying the positive as well as the negative ROL of ongoing investments in corporate learning contributes to a greater understanding the organization itself and how it can achieve its strategic goals in the future.

CHAPTER 6

The Competitive Edge

Corporate learning is not just a tool for enhancing skill and productivity; it also serves as an agent that defines an organization's culture as a good place to work—that gives as much as it takes.
—Sam Su, Vice Chairman, Yum! Brands, Inc.; Chairman and CEO, Yum! Restaurants China, Shanghai

The Continuous Integration of Learning and Strategy (CILS) is a process proven to work for both large and small companies seeking to remain competitive and survive in the new global economic environment. In preceding chapters, we have discussed this changing landscape and the critical components that are required for an effective solution. We've also outlined situations where the model does not work and highlighted the investment return that is generated when it does. Given all of this information as context, what are the specific ways in which the CILS model provides a real competitive advantage? How can companies implementing the model expect to better address current business challenges and differentiate themselves for success and survival?

The increasing shortage of skilled and talented workers makes it imperative for managers and organizations to find, hire, develop, and retain top employees. To do this, the desired skills first need to be clearly defined. This definition is by the demands of the business strategy and priorities. Then, the company must determine whether to "make or buy" talent to satisfy those needs—that is, develop existing employees or go out and find new ones who already possess the requisite skills. Either way, retaining employees requires engaging them on the job. But, as Peter Cappelli writes in his book, *Why Good People Can't Get Jobs*, the open competition for other companies' people, once a rarity in business, is stronger than ever.

In this intense era of strategic poaching, there are four distinct areas of organizational behavior and leadership that are influenced by talent management and that companies need to conquer to gain a competitive edge. These are the talent war, the culture of excellence, manager effectiveness, and brand enhancement. When their contribution are combined, they form the key to success and survival. CILS is the key to implementing the full package by "making" top talent or creating a culture and perception conducive for "buying" and retaining it.

The Talent War

Workers with strong, unique, and in-demand skill sets are benefiting from a current buyers' hiring market (see Figure 6-1). So what are some of the factors that cause them to leave or stay?

Reputation

At the height of the industrial era, two to three generations ago, the primary objectives of employees were opportunity, compensation, and secure employment. In the current information age, where Generation Y, also known as Millennials (approximately 18–30 years of age), occupy a large percentage of the available workforce (and a dominant percentage in the next 10 years), a different set of

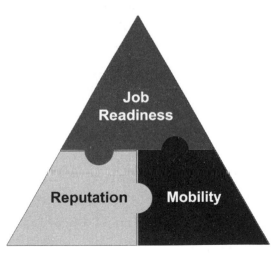

Figure 6-1 Elements of Talent Management

key objectives are prioritized—from work environment to flexibility to a reputation as "development friendly." company.

While most workers in the older Generation X and Baby Boomer generations have already matriculated far enough into their careers to have developed a respectable base set of skills, the Millennials are attracted to companies that are, at a minimum, perceived as strongly investing in the overall growth and career development trajectory of their staff. Millennials wonder: Is there a cultural focus in the company on giving to its people or taking from them? Millennials, in particular, want to know whether they will have the opportunity to develop a strong set of competencies and transferrable skills that can not only be useful now, for their current employer, but later on as well, as their careers develop. They are thinking about their futures and expecting to work now for companies that that will support that priority—whether they end up staying or leaving. Job cultures that have a reputation for extracting the best from their employees, only to replace them with more highly skilled and developed workers later, are perceived as far less attractive than those that have a reputation for injecting the best in transferrable skills and career development direction for their pool on a consistent basis. Companies using CILS as an operating model have prioritized learning as a key driver of strategy, so their need for developing people fuels a marketplace reputation that supports recruiting and retention.

In 2009, Melissa, then a 27-year-old computer programmer with bachelor's and master's degrees from two different Ivy League institutions, decided to test the job market. Her first two jobs had included a stint as an associate at a leading global British-based management consulting firm and one as a junior manager for a Brazilian-based petrochemical mid-market company. Her education, work experience, and unique/in-demand skill set made her a sought-after prospect across industries.

As Melissa searched for a new professional opportunity and responded to recruiting overtures (including from her current employer), she primarily focused on one question: "Will my new employer prepare me for senior management in my existing discipline? Aside from my role as a programmer, will I have the opportunity to learn the fundamentals of leadership, negotiations, and effective communications?"

Since responses and pitches from recruiters and hiring managers were largely indistinguishable across companies, Melissa relied on reputation to make her choice. Which companies had strong rankings in the "developing people" space? Which had been profiled in peer-reviewed or academic journals? Which companies had she heard good things about or seen/read about in the media related to this topic? What did her parents think? Her peer network? Ultimately, the reputation of a large U.S.-based technology and media company weighed in as the deciding vote of the recruiting war. She has since stayed with the company for five years, so they are also winning the retention war.

Job Readiness

Organizations that leverage the CILS model equip their employees with an enhanced ability and confidence to do their jobs. Developing staff in an ongoing cycle and ensuring that development is directly linked to corporate strategy (more specifically, divisional strategy and related individual requirements) keeps them well prepared to do their jobs.

Job retention is often influenced by three performance-related factors: ineffectiveness, failure, and/or burnout. When individuals do not obtain optimal effectiveness, it is typically the result of a lack of skill rather than any form of lack of engagement or effort. Not being prepared skill-wise to do a job creates a performance dynamic that puts an employees' position at risk for a variety of reasons. First, the individual stress of working hard but not executing at the highest level is frustrating for the individual because he or she is not realizing results that match efforts. Second, the employee's manager and team are frustrated due to a lack of acceptable contribution. In time, the ongoing gap in performance as a result of a lack of, or lack of an appropriate level of, necessary skills will lead to either burnout—the effect of trying extremely hard but remaining ineffective, or failure—the result of not getting the job done as required by positional requirements and expectations and being terminated.

For organizations that utilize a CILS approach, job readiness is built into the operating plan for all employees. Since development is tied to strategy, individuals, in practice, remain skilled and prepared to perform their roles—thus supporting and enhancing retention rates.

Jeff was an administrative assistant for a partner in a Chicago-based national accounting firm. His division experienced tremendous growth over the last several quarters, and his manager's new responsibility was to increase the size of the team by 15 percent. Part of Jeff's added responsibility, in turn, was to partner with a manager from the recruiting team to source potential applicants and manage preliminary screening processes. Given the volume of applicants, Jeff's responsibility with the recruiting effort escalated beyond the intended scope.

Since Jeff's experience and skills with the leading social media applications was limited, he struggled to source, sort, analyze, and communicate with the pool. He proved to be less than effective with the hiring project and, in the process, sacrificed quality on his baseline projects and responsibilities as well. The struggle persisted for nearly a year when Jeff's manager, realizing that the continuing surge in business would require ongoing sourcing support, decided to replace Jeff with a an assistant from another company who had a strong social media background. The impact on Jeff was clearly devastating. The impact on the organization was more significant than expected, given the time involved to onboard a new person into a complex and nuanced culture. If Jeff's older firm had utilized a CILS approach at the outset of this process, a proper course of training would have been assessed and implemented to support the strategic recruiting effort—and Jeff would have stayed in his job.

Mobility

In addition to wanting to work for a company that has a stellar reputation for developing people and actually working for one that keeps its employees properly skilled to perform strategic roles, the third talent need for a competitive advantage is to prepare workers for new roles in the organization. Generationally, we are seeing a shift in employees' commitments to staying along a certain track for their entire care paths. For example, in previous generations, someone may have started as a law clerk, moved on to be an associate, and followed the step path to partner. Today, Millennials may commit to the law firm for several years, then jump off the partner track to pursue a new career in business development at a corporation or in human resources management at a boutique hedge fund. Similarly, a Baby Boomer who has enjoyed a hallmark career in banking may seek a new opportunity to design and analyze community-based philanthropic programs. Both cases represent a handicapped position in the war for talent—losing key personnel due to a change of interest in role or responsibility.

Because the CILS model is continuously developing staff for strategic objectives—both directly tied to their current role as well as preparing them for future or expanded opportunities— internal mobility is a more readily available alternative to losing key talent.

Carmella was a Baby Boomer banker considering either retirement or a complete restart of her career. She decided to go back to school to learn new skills and obtained a certificate in Community Program Management. She proceeded to reengage the workforce as a program manager for a local foundation the provided guide dogs to visually impaired children. Now, if the investment bank where she had spent her entire 24-year career had prepared her to expand her skill base (even in the last couple years of her career), she could have stayed with the firm and provided her services to its own community foundation. In this case, she would still have been available as a resource to her former divisional colleagues, and she could have leveraged her talent and capability set for the company in a way that was financially and culturally beneficial to her native organization.

Culture of Excellence

As mentioned in Chapter 4, culture can be a barrier to integrating learning and strategy. It can also be the source of competitive advantage. A true culture of excellence is one that leverages CILS to provide an environment where preparation, adaptability, and ongoing support to do a job well are ever present (see Figure 6-2).

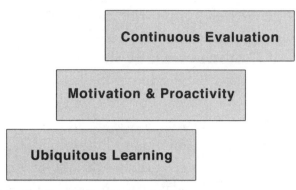

Figure 6-2   Building Blocks of Cultural Excellence

Ubiquitous Learning

When learning is ever present, ongoing, and broadly distributed throughout the entire organization, the level of support raises the bar for preparation, goal setting, and performance. A level of pride exists when employees exceed performance expectations because they have been prepared and supported to do just that. In fact, since everyone has been exposed to, and benefited from, the CILS process, a level of internal competition typically develops above and beyond the self-imposed excellence marker. In a natural context, employees are always seeking to find opportunities to surpass the performance of their peers.

In a culture of excellence, this competitive jousting starts at a high level, thereby yielding results that are much more impressive. The constant production of this type of high-level work product leads to a variety of positive, yet unintended, benefits. The most notable are out-of-the box contributions that emerge in the process. So, instead of just getting the work done, the culture transforms into a field of innovation, where new ideas, concepts, and recommendations are actually competing and advancing individual and collective innovation well beyond the expected.

A marketing and communications team for a television production company in Brisbane was preparing for the announcement and launch campaign of a new anchor and news team. Instead of storyboarding the approach and synching a countdown schedule, as is normally done for this type of project, the team of 46 people ended up managing a contest to rank and score the plethora of ideas that were generated by individuals and subgroups on the team. The training that team members had received over the years in relation to various strategic projects prepared them, for example, on how to conduct benchmark analyses and comparative assessments, map scenario plans for alternative approaches, and create mixed-media segment shorts for advertising across channels. As a result of the continuous learning of the team, the level of energy and creativity displayed for this project was exciting and produced an end-stage plan that was much more innovative and cutting edge than would have been present absent a CILS culture.

Motivation and Proactivity

CILS creates an ongoing investment in the training of its people. As the organization benefits, the people benefit.

The people, however, understand that this type of investment is not common and truly appreciate the opportunity and commitment the company shows to their development. This appreciation is minimally expressed by a heightened level of engagement at work. That is, employees are more excited to be on the job, more excited to participate, and more excited to collaborate and execute an excellent work product. This type of motivation has a partially subjective measure, but it also results in quantifiable performance increases. Employees who are motivated work harder, longer, and with more directed focus.

Appreciation for the investment in learning also leads to a level of inspiration and motivation in individuals and teams that extends beyond traditional work assignments. In other words, appreciation motivates them to independently explore strategies and tactics, outside of their domain and scope of responsibility, that will allow them to "pay back" by way of providing an unexpected competitive edge.

An example is not when a worker creates improved, streamlined efficiencies in a production cycle or when that employee plugs a hole in a legal case with a new and insightful analysis. Rather, an example is when an employee in the facilities management department takes it upon herself to analyze staffing inefficiencies in the compensation and benefits group, develops an implementation model, and shares findings and recommendations with key stakeholders. Again, this type of targeted proactivity is the result an appreciation for continuous access to learning and development, which further supports Chapter 5's return on learning premise.

Cultures that consist of employees who appreciate the investment and benefits of CILS on their careers have a foundation of excellence that is supported by motivated engagement and proactive innovation.

Continuous Evaluation

The ongoing integration of strategy and learning promotes the continuous evaluation of performance rather just an annual or other term period assessment review. These approaches differ in a number of ways. A continuous evaluation starts by analyzing strengths and skill gaps to identify the relationship between positional objectives and a staff member's level of expertise. Because it is continuous, these strengths and weaknesses can be evaluated on a project-by-project basis—in real time and with direct relevance. The excellence attributes are recognized, positively reinforced, and occasionally rewarded at the time of incident. Gap assessments are translated into performance improvement plans that link and match relevant learning and development efforts to drive new skill adoption and quickly close the gap.

Annual evaluations also identify skill mastery and gaps and determine respective strategies for exploiting and/or closing them, but since the period spans a defined cycle, the attributes are often communicated as general themes and lack specific examples. Recommendations are more generalized and not targeted to specific tasks, initiatives, projects, and expected outcomes.

Deborah is a systems engineer in the refrigeration division of a compressor and automated solutions manufacturer in Nordborg, Denmark. As the lead project manager on a number of engagements featuring outsourced providers, Deborah was challenged with critical contracting specifications including scope definitions, time and cost projections, and deliverable penalties. As part of an ongoing evaluation and development process, Deborah's difficulty was diagnosed after just one vendor/contract difficulty. A customized and intensive training curriculum and program was developed for Deborah and delivered over the course of a few hour-long sessions during one week. The following six contract negotiations and management cycles were incident free, and her gap was officially rendered "closed."

The CILS process not only allows for the direct, real-time focus on skill positioning, but it helps to appropriately weight focus directly on positive attributes and improvement categories in a timely manner versus permitting the unintended reinforcement and proliferation of bad behavior. Conducted on a regular basis and in line with new assignments and new expectations, employees are constantly aware of performance mastery as well as areas of improvement and constantly provided with the support to improve and advance.

Manager Effectiveness

One of the most significant benefits of CILS for competitive advantage is that of manager effectiveness, which, in this context, is the ability of leaders in an organization to influence, communicate, and drive performance for subordinates, peers, and managers alike. The leadership and management within an organization drive the culture and performance and, when operating effectively through CILS, create a sustainable competitive advantage. Senior leaders, unit leaders, and peer leaders can all have a substantial influence on an effective management culture—if they are actively linking strategy and learning (see Figure 6-3).

C-Suite

The CILS model requires an astute and thorough strategic planning process. Since a learning organization can only tie a framework of development to strategy, a strategy needs to be in place for the connection to take place. Again, the learning function should be part of the strategy-setting process to (1) inform strategy insights and analysis about the talent profile of the organization, including its skill capabilities and engagement patterns; and (2) validate the reality of matching strategic priorities with learning initiatives and programs based on resources, timing, and saturation.

In the past, and in some smaller markets and industries today, a company could survive by responding to market

Figure 6-3 Targets of Managerial Influence

conditions and maintaining a fluid, nimble, and reactive response to doing business. Even if no short- or long-term plans were developed, these companies were able to compete and survive based on a tactical approach. This type of reactive approach in today's market makes it almost impossible to directly integrate learning. As such, the potential competitive advantage of managerial leadership is lost.

When senior leaders in the C-suite use CILS to develop short-, mid-, and long-term plans for growth, market positioning, structural alignment, and competitive analysis, the result is an aggressive and highly competitive operating strategy. The process of using the learning enterprise to inform and build the plan ensures that a thorough process was followed and considerations of all aspects of the business were conducted—from people to infrastructure to competitors to resourcing.

Once a CILS plan is created and adopted, the impact on other aspects of business in the C-suite is beneficial, further adding to the competitive value proposition. With a clear strategy and a clear plan for correlating people development and efficient execution, communication with key constituencies such as the board of directors, shareholders, and the media are more productive as well. Each of these constituencies can better support the goals of the company with a clear articulation of direction and ongoing success based on clear focus of people and their performance by way of development.

Business Unit

Once an overarching strategic plan is in place via C-suite leadership, business unit managers are positioned to provide a competitive advantage through substrategy priorities and execution plans. If properly trained, business leaders are then poised to create real value and a competitive advantage for their companies.

Business leaders often rise through the ranks to senior-level positions by being effective individual contributors. Early in their careers, they excel at adding commercial value individually and thus are quickly and consecutively promoted up the chain. For leaders who progressed in this way, the problem is that many never learned how to actually lead. Since they often weren't promoted based on exemplary managerial skills, they never honed competencies such as effectively communicating expectations, creating followership, leading without authority, building and motiving a diverse work force, and delegating for maximum scalability.

For business leaders who emerged as "commercial killers" en route to management in CILS organizations, the outcomes are very different. In these cases, the process helped managers develop the aforementioned key attributes in addition to setting subgoals based on company strategy, identifying gaps/needs and aligning support, maintaining an ongoing evaluation of performance, and consistently rewarding and recognizing excellence objectively.

Simon is a sales manager for an enterprise software company based in Walldorf, Germany. For ten consecutive years, Simon individually led all B-to-B executed transactions and even outperformed his next closest colleague by a margin of at least 10 percent. Following such a string of unparalleled individual successes and a quick, successive string of regional and territory manager assignments, Simon was promoted to European sales manager with responsibility for 120 relationship managers and over one-third of the total company revenue.

With limited time in a management seat, it could easily be assumed that Simon's core competency was sales and not management. However, in his time with the company, Simon had consistently and continuously participated in a wide range of learning initiatives geared toward management and leadership. The company's intention, through years of training, was to prepare him for a management role by equipping him with the necessary skills and tools to transition seamlessly when the time came. As it turns out, Simon's transition was successful as evidenced by evaluation scores, attrition rates, and overall team performance.

Managers and Peers

In addition to leading and influencing subordinate staff, key constituents, and stakeholders, managers at all levels in an organization provide a competitive edge when they also influence their managers and peers. In *Leading Up: Managing Your Boss So You Can Both Win*, Michael Useem describes how leaders need to lead up, a necessary strategy when a supervisor is micromanaging rather than macrothinking, when a division head offers clear directives but can't see the future, or when shareholders demand instant gain but need long-term growth. Once again, these tactics only work when managers learn how to use them in practice. Continuous learning against strategy is key.

Anwat joined a medical informatics laboratory in Columbia, Missouri, as its new CFO. After participating in several rounds of strategic planning and witnessing the culture of CILS in the organization, Anwat recognized that a different approach for communicating certain "sticky" topics to the board (such as attrition rates, compensation trends, and insurance coverage and fees) would facilitate less contentious committee sessions, expedite decision making, and create unanimous support for a greater number of key initiatives. Following leading-up strategies learned in training on the job, Anwat convinced his CEO to make a few bold, yet analytically prudent, changes to the board's communication and outreach approach. After essentially reengaging the governing constituency body, Anwat's action showed another way that CILS can initiate competitive opportunity.

Managers across levels, functions, and tenure can provide value to their peer counterparts in two distinct ways: (1) through coaching and (2) by upholding accountability standards. Peer-to-peer counsel in the form of coaching is often a safer way to solicit feedback on performance or actions, get advice on key decision points, or receive strategies on approaches for taking action. As with other manager effectiveness strategies, peer coaching requires training in order for exchanges to have maximum benefit.

Peer managers are also an ideal source for providing honest and authentic, yet informal, counsel related to upholding certain standards of accountability. As a manager, who is watching you? Who is making sure your management behavior is effective? If the performance on your team is slipping mid-quarter, who is going to challenge you to uphold your share of the load? And, who will serve as a consistent voice of recommendation regarding your own personal development needs (timing, area of focus, etc.)?

Overall, in order for the benefits of manager effectiveness to have the influence and impact to drive competitive advantage, managers must have access to development on the subtleties of use.

Brand Enhancement

Maintaining a CILS approach not only provides an edge for talent, culture, and management, but it also has the potential to dramatically influence the brand value for internal and external stakeholders (see Figure 6-4).

Internal Ambassadors

As mentioned earlier, staff who appreciate the existence of CILS in the workplace operating culture are more likely to be motivated to remain consistently engaged, innovate, and drive creativity beyond the boundaries of expectations. Those appreciative staff will also serve as the principal ambassadors in promoting the benefits of the CILS culture to any and all curious constituents outside of the company. Whether the audience is engaged in a social or professional setting, the ambassadorial message of investment,

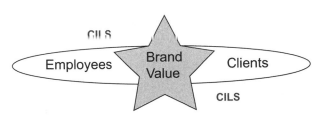

Figure 6-4   Brand Value Proposition

development, and results will resonate and raise the profile of the organization. The staff who live it are the best and most credible spokespersons.

Client Value Proposition

When the external audience that learns about the extraordinary CILS culture is a client, then a dual benefit ensues. First, the perception of the organization is raised. Consumers and customers link product and/or service quality with the environmental conditions in which those products and services were developed and cultivated. In other words, if the business runs that well, the output must be comparatively superb. The subsequent client satisfaction results in an enhancement of service—more and regular contracted work and potentially some best-practice sharing around CILS optimization.

Finally, internal ambassador and client testimonials typically lead to editorial accolades and recognition, which provide external validation for excellence.

Summary

In order to succeed in business, a company needs to have a competitive edge in the marketplace. Gone are the days when just having a superior product or lower prices or more market penetration formed the basis of a company's competitive edge. An organization needs to get its house in order and become a proactive learning organization committed to the progressive tools afforded by the CILS method. Corporate learning initiatives serve to bolster four of the strongest paths to success: the talent war, a culture of excellence, manager effectiveness, and brand enhancement. Through an ongoing dedication to the CILS values of analysis, strategic planning, and continuous assessment, evaluation, and programmatic learning, all members of a learning organization from the C-suite to middle management to the rank and file employees work together to give the company an edge on the competition.

CHAPTER 7

Integration in Practice: Comcast and Sears

Companies must now realize that strategic priorities are nothing more than intended actions; simultaneous development in people in support of those priorities is essential for any results to be sustained.
—David Levin, CEO, McGraw-Hill Education, New York

*L*earning to Succeed has focused on how the ever-changing environmental context and business landscape have redefined the rules for corporate success. Competitive advantage and survival depend on an "integration formula" and "programming framework" that allow the business planning process to leverage learning and development as a strategic counterpart for implementation. Although there are significant barriers to implementing an effective Continuous Integration of Learning and Strategy (CILS) process, the potential return on investment and, indeed, the necessity for success justify the need for prioritized focus in this area.

Throughout the preceding chapters, topical vignettes have served as examples to illustrate best practices in adopting the CILS-based approach. Both small and large companies, across industries and around the globe, have been highlighted to showcase individual and organizational examples of failure and success. Regardless of the approach or outcome, however, it is clear that an increasing number of global organizations and individuals are realizing the need for the integration of learning and strategy in an exhaustive range of situations. For the field to continue to advance toward more effective solutions, we must identify and study existing best practices in the field. What does CILS-based success look like? What process was used to achieve it? What were the outcomes?

Two cases that highlight comprehensive and longitudinal CILS are the Comcast Corporation and Sears Holdings. By responding to time-sensitive environmental and market conditions, devising a competitive strategic response, and integrating a linked learning solution, both have realized short- and long-term success that supports the core of operational practices and outlines how key components in the strategic process can be utilized to create a winning solution.

Comcast Corporation

The Company

Comcast Corporation (NASDAQ: CMCSA) is a global media and technology company with two primary businesses, Comcast Cable and NBCUniversal. Comcast Cable is the nation's largest video, high-speed Internet, and phone provider to residential customers under the XFINITY brand; it also provides these services to businesses. NBCUniversal operates 30 news, entertainment, and sports cable networks, the NBC and Telemundo broadcast networks, television production operations, television station groups, Universal Pictures, and Universal Parks and Resorts.

In February 2014, the company announced its pending merger with Time Warner Cable, the second largest cable company in the United States.

The Context

The financial crisis of 2007–2008 resulted in the threat or total collapse of large financial institutions, the bailout of banks by the national government, and downturns in stock markets around the world. In many areas, the housing market also suffered, resulting in evictions, foreclosures, and prolonged unemployment. The crisis played a significant role in the failure of key businesses, declines in consumer wealth estimated in the trillions of U.S. dollars, and an overall downturn in economic activity leading to the 2008–2012 global recession.

Against this backdrop, in 2009, the senior leadership at Comcast decided to prioritize strategic objectives by identifying and analyzing two key areas:

- Company-wide inefficiencies in the operating processes
- Opportunities to enhance the customer service experience, performance, and related quality components

The purpose of the first mandate was to ensure that opportunities for conducting business with maximum efficiency were identified—a tall order given an already high-functioning, productive cross-divisional operating record. The purpose of the second mandate was to double-down focus on providing a best-in-class overall client experience—particularly as loyal customers faced distressed conditions in their personal and professional lives in the midst of global market shifts.

The Process

In response to senior leadership's call to action, an opportunity to address both focal areas was identified in connection with learning and development. By centralizing company-wide programs and initiatives under Comcast University, quality would not only be maintained, but enhanced, while simultaneously creating greater efficiency in the overall function. Further, the function could then be better positioned to serve as the focal point for training targeted staff on enhanced customer service strategies and techniques.

Prior to 2009, the learning function at Comcast used a decentralized model—allowing training to initiate from multiple owners within the business units. In other words, the responsibility for training was distributed between and among Comcast University and each individual business unit or even subgroup in some cases. While business and learning objectives were satisfied and program quality level was consistently rated as average to good, efficiencies were lost in the process.

Given the decentralization, Comcast University's role was diffuse and fragmented. Massive duplication existed as evidenced by:

- Multiple reporting relationships for learning professionals largely doing the same type of work. For example, there were 90 different reporting relationships across the decentralized learning organization, but only 36 out of 750 learning professionals reported to the Chief Learning Officer (CLO).
- Multiple editions of courses available on singular topics. For example, 39 different courses existed across the company related to street pole service, but there are only three ways to climb a pole! Further, there were 109 different new hire courses available for call center representatives.

Under the decentralized model, Comcast University also held responsibilities for functions beyond learning and development (L&D), including such tasks as:

- Managing vehicles
- Ordering tires
- Managing data not related to L&D

To address the efficiency issues and create an infrastructure to enhance customer service training, Comcast decided to centralize the L&D function.

The Solution/Integration

Centralization of all of learning and development activities under Comcast University emanated from two critical factors: top leadership sponsorship and a link to key business priorities.

From a governance standpoint, Comcast established a new National Learning Council with the charge of linking strategic priorities on an ongoing and continuous basis with learning needs and determining related resourcing and sponsorship (i.e., the CILS model). The Council is cochaired by the Chief Operating Officer (COO) of Comcast, David L. Watson, and the Chief Learning Officer, Martha Soehren. Members of the Council include all product executive vice presidents plus presidents of geographic divisions.

Structurally, the integration solution led to a shift in reporting such that all learning professionals in the organization now report to the CLO. And, all learning-related resources also became centralized through the office of the CLO, with the strategic hypothesis being that a consistent learning experience drives a consistent customer experience.

The inaugural operational activity of the newly structured Comcast University was a company-wide audit. The first assessment uncovered more than 25,000 learning objects and courses across the company. Subsequent structuring and alignment allowed for organization of activities, reduction in redundancies, and an improved process for reporting on how much learning is taking place, how much it is costing the company, and where to allocate available resources for new support.

The inaugural program activity of the newly structured Comcast University was the first high-potential development program for hourly employees. Immediately, the program resulted in 90 percent retention of a critical population and prompted a 65 percent promotion rate in some markets.

The Benefits/Success

Five years after the strategic shift, Comcast University operates as one of the top functions in the world, focusing on leadership development, learning solutions, and talent management.

Within the business, the role has changed from "taking orders" or even duplicating efforts to one of a strategic partner focused on using learning techniques to solve real-time business challenges. Now, there is consensus alignment with business partners — speaking their "language" and understanding their issues. As a result, active participation from senior leaders across the board is at a historical high — largely based on the realized value of the strategic integration of programs. This is evidenced by the fact that some new programming initiatives are funded in the first year by the business units, and then added to the budget by the Council for subsequent years.

This year, Comcast University will deliver 4.6 million hours of training—13 percent of which is virtual/online. For example, call center training is conducted through a portal that leverages a "blended" solution that includes classroom sessions, online modules, games, and role-plays.

For all of its offerings, Comcast University tracks the productivity and quality of the instructors and sessions. The ongoing goal is to realize 80 to 100 percent productivity for assigned platform time. Internal customer feedback has improved a half letter grade every year since centralization. And, aggregated data shows an marked improvement in the customer experience following targeted training. Quality, quantity (scalability), and efficiency are all focal points of the function.

To measure ongoing impact, Comcast University maintains a cycle that includes implementing solutions, measuring their effects, sharing transactional data, and sharing impact stories. The cycle continuously increases credibility, which in turn increases business partners' use, followed by employee improved performance and end-user (client) benefit.

Summary

The primary premise of this book is to show how and why the CILS process is necessary for contemporary organizations to gain competitive advantage. This case shows how Comcast demonstrated the benefits of CILS through an integrated approach that linked strategy and learning to address two key priorities.

The centralization of all learning efforts under Comcast University resulted in the desired efficiency, as well as quality control objectives. Efficiency operations were enhanced as duplicate offerings were consolidated and gaps in developed needs were filled. Further, service objectives, such as improved customer experience protocols and behavior, resulted in more consistent excellence across the enterprise.

Sears Holdings

The Company

Sears Holdings Corporation (NASDAQ: SHLD) is a leading integrated retailer focused on seamlessly connecting the digital and physical shopping experiences to serve its members—wherever, whenever, and however they want to shop. Sears Holdings is home to Shop Your Way®, a social shopping platform offering members rewards for shopping at Sears and Kmart, as well as with other retail partners across categories important to them. The company operates through its subsidiaries, including Sears, Roebuck and Co. and Kmart Corporation, with full-line and specialty retail stores across the United States.

The Context

Sears Holdings was formed in 2005 when Sears, Roebuck and Co. (founded in 1886) merged with the Kmart Corporation (founded in 1962), bringing together two companies with longstanding histories and proud heritages, but with differing cultures and operations. In order to accelerate the transformation of the new enterprise as a whole, a distributed leadership model was put in place dividing operations into more than 30 business units. This operating model enabled leaders of each business unit to exercise greater control, authority, and autonomy and make changes at a much faster rate, but it also created unique challenges for L&D.

In addition, the new enterprise strategy focused on an integrated retailing model that seamlessly connects the customer experience across all touch points, whether digital or physical. This required a significant investment in new digital technologies and platforms, including upgrading online and mobile platforms for Sears and Kmart, as well as for the Kenmore and Craftsman brands, and the creation of the social shopping platform Shop Your Way. A new culture of innovation, agile product development, and rapid change grew up around these technology teams, thereby further increasing the need for adaptive, just-in-time L&D solutions.

After the merger, functional and technical training was further decentralized across the business units, which helped increase the speed of implementation of this type of learning content. However, it also reduced the resources available centrally to support the transformation at an enterprise level. Sears Holdings University, once the source of the majority of L&D for Sears, was relegated to a minor role in soft skills training and ultimately was disbanded. By the start of 2012, L&D was no longer a key lever supporting the centralized strategy of the company.

The Process

In order to revitalize the centralized learning function at Sears Holding as a strategic lever supporting the objectives of the enterprise as a whole, a change in focus and strategy had to take place. Due to the highly differentiated learning needs across the major business units, it made sense to continue with decentralized support for functional and technical training. What was needed, centrally, was a renewed focus on the core strategy of the enterprise and an approach to L&D that could connect individualized learning needs to the core needs of the business and provide learning solutions that could scale across all business units at Sears Holdings.

The foundation for a new strategic approach to L&D was built upon four primary elements:

- Alignment on the overall objectives of the enterprise
- Identification of the strategic leadership competencies needed to support those objectives
- Creation of a mechanism to rapidly and continuously identify learning and development needs

- Implementation of a scalable platform that connects associates with learning content that continually refreshes to meet to their individual needs

The Solution/Integration

In late 2012, Dean Carter, Chief Human Resources Officer at Sears Holdings, led an effort to identify a new company mission and a shared set of key results as part of a broader initiative to transform the culture at Sears Holdings. The mission and key results were refined over the coming months under the new leadership of Eddie Lampert, who took over the CEO role in early 2013. Ultimately, a simple mission statement and four key results were identified that gave every associate, from the frontline cashier to the business unit leader, a direct line of sight to the ultimate purpose of their work at the company and a common language around what matters most.

This strategic shift launched the first companywide training initiative that had taken place since the merger. More than 200,000 associates at Sears Holdings went through a classroom training session (that included blended elements for remote workers) to ensure all associates understood the new culture and could see the link between their roles and the four key results of the company. Each business unit describes how its work supports one or more of the key results, and associates link their individual priorities each year directly to the four key results. This was the first element in laying the foundation for the transformation of L&D at Sears Holdings.

The second element that Carter and his team put in place was a new enterprise leadership model. The model was created through the direct input from Lampert and other senior leaders. It was further refined through in-depth analytics conducted on several years of executive assessment data that identified the competencies most predictive of business results at Sears Holdings. The final model included 14 leadership competencies grouped into four broad categories. At Sears Holdings, the belief is that anyone, anywhere, can lead, so the model was further defined at six levels in the company:

- Three levels of managers of others
- Three levels for individual contributors

The result is that all associates can see the behaviors expected of them at their level and enjoy full transparency into what they would need to develop and demonstrate in order to advance into higher levels of leadership in the company. This common view into leadership laid a foundation for a common set of L&D resources across the enterprise.

The third element provided a mechanism for continually identifying learning needs, which is especially critical in helping associates keep up with the rapidly changing demands and new technologies that are necessary to drive the business transformation. In 2014, Sears Holdings replaced its traditional annual performance review process with continuous crowd-sourced feedback. Associates now have a digital cloud-based application they can access from any device with Internet access, including their computer or store terminals and their smart phones, that allows them to request and give feedback to or from anyone else on the platform. Most Sears stores now have iPads that also power the platform. E-mail notifications let associates read their feedback or see requests as soon as they arrive. They can then quickly link back to the tool, which drives ongoing engagement with the platform. Associates receive training on how to give helpful and relevant feedback to others in general, as well as how to offer specific tips and techniques for giving certain types of feedback, such as upward feedback.

One of the categories associates obtain feedback on through the new tool is how they are demonstrating the competencies that make up the enterprise leadership model. In order to quickly translate feedback into insights and action, each associate has continuous access to a personal dashboard of their feedback within the tool, which includes a simple bar chart summarizing their feedback on the leadership model. The chart displays areas of strength, as well as areas of development that would add the greatest value to the business. Managers receive training on how to help associates arrive at their own insights from the feedback tool. The goal is to instill a forward-looking growth mindset in associates and let them take control of their development. Managers and Human Resource business partners are also given access to the aggregated feedback results through team level dashboards. With over 10,000 pieces of real-time feedback flowing through the tool each month, this enables a new level in learning needs analysis, an evergreen look as the leadership development needs for anyone or any team at any level at any time.

The fourth element needed to bring the other three together and close the loop between development and business results was the implementation of a scalable learning platform. Sears has had some form of a traditional learning management system for over a decade, but in late 2014 a new gamified learning management system was launched on the same broader platform that houses the crowd-sourced feedback tool. This new learning tool has the ability to provide targeted learning interactions reinforced through gamification. Complete with points, badges, and leaderboards, these gamified elements provides much needed stickiness and appeal for associates, while also enabling a way to deliver targeted learning needs. By linking the data coming in everyday from the crowd-sourced feedback tool, Sears Holdings can featuring certain learning content more than others, adjusting the point values to motivate actions or simply suggesting or pushing learning content onto individual learning plans. The result is that all associates receive a personalized view to the learning platform and personalized learning content informed by what others are observing about their behaviors and the areas of development that would drive the greatest value. The linkage between learning content and feedback works the other way too, enabling analytics that quickly identify the best learning content based on whether it actually leads to an observable change in behaviors seen in subsequent crowd-sourced feedback across the population.

The Benefits/Success

The net result of these efforts over the past two years has been the revitalization of centralized learning at Sears Holdings, centered on the overall enterprise mission and built to address the specific needs of the company during this period of accelerating transformation and investment in new technologies. By leveraging new macro trends in performance and learning, including continuous crowd-sourced feedback, gamification, and social and mobile interactions enabled though a new technology platform, the centralized learning function was able to:

- Support an enterprise-wide mandate to innovate and revolutionize the service model and provide an integrated, customer experience in the new technological age.
- Create a common understanding of leadership at Sears Holdings and support continuous learning and development for any associate at any level who wants to grow as a leader, while still allowing for business unit decentralization and control.
- Provide flexible, just-in-time access to learning content that is specifically targeted to each individual learner's needs through the linkage of continuous crowd-sourced feedback and the learning management system.

The result is faster skill development, growth, and much more direct link to company results.

Summary

Sears Holdings needed to find a way to revitalize the centralized learning function as a strategic lever supporting the objectives of the enterprise as a whole and supporting the business transformation that was taking place. What was needed centrally was a renewed focus on the core strategy built upon four primary elements:

- Alignment on the overall objectives of the enterprise
- Identification of the strategic leadership competencies needed to support those objectives
- Creation of a mechanism to rapidly and continuously identify learning and development needs
- Implementation of a scalable platform that could connect associates with learning content that continually refreshes to meet to their individual needs

When combined, these four elements make up a learning ecosystem at Sears Holdings that allows the centralized learning function to develop and curate new learning content based on the most pressing needs of the business and then rapidly to deploy it on a wide scale across the enterprise.

APPENDIX

Executive Perspectives: Deloitte and Procter & Gamble

Global corporations that seek competitive transformation require a deliberate and long-term commitment to continuous learning. Quick results are not to be expected, but sustained advantage is the desired outcome.
—Adil Popat, CEO, Simbacorp, Nairobi

As Adil Popat highlights above, executives' understanding of the core elements of learning and leadership development in organizations is fundamental to realizing sustainable performance improvement. And, as discussed, those executives must at once directly participate in, and have influence over, the strategic agenda setting process, have deep subject matter expertise in cross-functional learning disciplines, and possess multicycle experience executing complex, integrated operational plans.

Deloitte LLP (Deloitte) and Procter & Gamble (P&G) are both critically acclaimed learning organizations that possess all of the necessary aforementioned elements of leadership and practice.

Deloitte, LLP

Deloitte, LLP, is one of the "big-four" global professional services firms based in New York City. By revenue and number of professionals, it is the largest professional services network in the world. With more than 200,000 professionals in over 150 countries, its offers audit, tax, consulting, enterprise risk, and financial advisory services. In fiscal year 2013–2014, Deloitte earned approximately $34.2 billion in revenue.

Below is an excerpt from a recent discussion with Punit Renjen, Chairman, and Craig Gill, Chief Learning Officer (CLO), that focused on Deloitte's experience as a learning organization and its efforts to fully integrate with strategy:

What defines a learning-organization orientation for a company? In other words, how does the company know when it is ready for integration?

For an organization to become oriented toward learning, leadership must believe that investing in their people is core to their culture (who they are) and essential to their business strategy (where they are going). In an economy increasingly dominated by applied knowledge, success depends on attracting, developing, and deploying professionals who can out-think their competitors. At Deloitte, we believe that to deliver the best possible services for our clients' toughest challenges, we must accelerate how our people learn, adapt, and grow. So for us, integrating learning into our business strategy is a given.

What does it mean for a learning executive (senior-most executive responsible for learning and development) role to be meaningfully integrated with the CEO and the Board?

Sustaining a business culture and strategy in which learning is a priority requires a significant investment. This includes expenses for courses, travel, and facilities, as well as the considerable time and attention of leaders facilitating the learning programs and the professionals participating in them.

As learning experiences are expanded outside the classroom, the organization must allocate additional resources. Given this level of investment, the CLO must not only be adept in applying learning practices to accelerate performance, he or she must also possess the business acumen to connect actions with strategy and demonstrate business returns for the senior-most leaders of the organization. In turn, senior management and the Board must involve the CLO in strategy formulation so that learning is "built in" to strategic and operational plans. At Deloitte, for example, the CLO was fully involved in the $300M strategic decision that led to the investment in Deloitte University and is an integral part of our business operational leadership team.

How can a learning executive develop and deepen a foundation of trust within a company in order to facilitate strategy and learning integration initiatives?

First and foremost, the organization's culture and business strategy must place a priority on investing in its people—the CLO alone cannot be responsible for demonstrating the value of an integrated learning strategy. However, the CLO is instrumental in creating an effective strategy and executing it. He or she builds trust with the organization's senior management as well as with its people by acting as a performance improvement consultant—asking the probing questions and getting the facts to diagnose and recommend the right set of actions to deliver sustainable improvements.

Sometimes this requires courage and persuasion to convince managers to look beyond the convenient action of creating a new learning course and to instead execute a disciplined series of actions that may include on-the-job actions and reinforcing leadership behaviors.

How can a learning executive maximize coordination with stakeholders, both internal and external?

The effective CLO actively builds networks both within the organization and externally. Internally, the CLO can maintain alignment with business goals by convening a learning council comprising senior leaders from across the organization. The agenda should focus on strategy execution (or adaptation), priorities and results.

The CLO's external networks bring thought leadership and best practices into the organization. In the process, these relationships reinforce the organization's talent brand in the marketplace, including with customers and academic institutions. One example of this is the Deloitte University Leadership Center for Clients, which is a catalyst for exchanging best practices from within Deloitte, and across business, government, and academia.

How can the learning executive distill knowledge both up and down the information chain of the company?

Sharing and leveraging knowledge throughout an organization is increasingly complex as the volume and pace of information expands exponentially. The CLO can tap critical knowledge throughout the organization by equipping more tenured professionals to be teachers (in the classroom) and capitalizing on daily learning opportunities (outside the classroom).

For instance, a key principle of Deloitte's learning strategy is utilizing the "leader-as-teacher" model throughout the formal learning curriculum, using partners and senior professionals as facilitators in the classroom. Once back "on the job" at a client engagement, this experience also reinforces our strong emphasis on mentorship because our leaders use those teaching skills to apprentice less-tenured team members. These actions serve to connect the strategic mission—helping clients address their most complex challenges—with the accelerated skills and knowledge individuals and teams need to deliver on the strategy.

Once incubated, how can companies institutionalize the inclusion of learning plans in corporate strategies?

An organization that is committed to investing in its people will always include learning as a key component of its talent strategy. It is important to institutionalize an effective strategy-development process that is grounded in the talent strategy, examines business and environmental forces five-to-ten years out that could affect talent—and specifically learning—plans, and then crystalizes choices and actions.

The strategic talent plan is a key tool for the Board and senior management to ensure that annual business plans are aimed at achieving both short- and longer term priorities.

How can companies ensure that recommendations for initiatives are data driven?

Like any strategy, effective learning strategies and decisions must be based upon facts and rigorous analysis. One approach is to utilize a strategic learning decision model where learning actions are clustered along a continuum of requirements. At Deloitte, the base of the continuum includes operational needs, such as maintaining the technical knowledge and licensing required to conduct business in a regulated environment. Another example is on-boarding new professionals to deliver excellent client service.

The decision criteria for implementing such initiatives are highly quantitative, including quality, cost, and timeliness. In contrast, farther along the continuum are more strategic, longer term needs, such as development of future organizational leaders. Decision criteria for implementing these types of initiatives typically factor in strategic business priorities, assessments of target leadership attributes, and gap analyses based on the current skills base.

How can companies ensure that measurement and reassessment of strategy/learning initiatives are ongoing?

Successful organizations make a habit of using the Plan–Do–Check–Act quality model—building regular checkpoints and course correction into operational and financial planning and management. At Deloitte, this same discipline extends to the critical business processes of talent management and learning. The talent and learning implications of business strategies are documented and initiatives are executed. As part of the regular business cycle, progress is reviewed and corrections made as necessary by senior management, with Board oversight. In this way, we ensure that learning investments remain aligned with strategic and operational plans, are efficiently executed, and are contributing to our ability to serve our clients with distinction and invest in our people for life.

Procter & Gamble Co.

Procter & Gamble Co. (NYSC: PG), is a multinational consumer goods company based in Cincinnati. Its products include pet foods, cleaning agents, and personal care items. Until recently, with the sale of Pringles to the Kellogg Company, its products also included foods and beverages. In fiscal year 2013–2014, Procter & Gamble (P&G) recorded $83.1 billion in revenue.

Below is a excerpt from a recent discussion with Dr. Ann E. Schulte, Global Leader of Learning and Leadership Development, on her vision for the Continuous Integration of Learning and Strategy and the related uses and practices at P&G.

What defines a learning-organization orientation for a company? In other words, how does the company know when it is ready for integration?

Companies are ready for a learning-organization orientation when they concede that talent is the most sustainable advantage in a global knowledge economy and their talent practices are central to business results and success.

Many companies acknowledge the need and recognize the importance of learning, but begin to call themselves learning organizations without a true understanding of what it means to have such an orientation. Most often, the moniker is mistakenly used when a firm places value on employee development. While support for individual learning and development is certainly a component of being a learning organization, it is no indication that the organization has put an emphasis on the management systems necessary to ensure the organization itself learns.

In 2008, the *Harvard Business Review* published an article by Garvin, Edmondson, and Gino asking, "Is Yours a Learning Organization" and proposing three building blocks to guide companies in pursuit of this orientation. The first calls for a company culture that provides a supportive learning environment, which the authors further specify as one that provides psychological safety, appreciation of differences, openness to new ideas, and time for reflection. The second building block requires establishing concrete learning process and practices and embedding them in the business. These practices relate to experimentation, information collection, analysis, education and training, and information transfer. The third building block is leadership that reinforces learning.

The authors have made their recommendation actionable by providing companies with a diagnostic survey tool that allows learning leaders to compare and analyze the more concrete segments of each building block. Companies, or units within them, can determine elements of a learning organization on which to focus attention, as well as benchmark their results against other firms that have used the diagnostic.

In my experience, intentions for all these building blocks are good, but the challenge lies in the realities of the fast pace of business. For example, consider the construct of reflection. Reflection, as in taking the time to think about what you are doing and how it relates to what you already know, is a cognitive process that needs intentional focus. Such focus requires time, and many employees do not take the time necessary for such processing, often because they do not believe such "quiet activity" will be recognized and supported. Instead, they power on to the next task or assignment. As a result, lessons and connections garnered through various experiences or in specific contexts may not get "recorded" by either the individual or the organization and, thus, learning fails to occur.

Companies that recognize the value of reflection to ensure such learning have to do more than tell employees it is permissible to take time for reflection. Management systems and cultural norms must encourage and support the practice. Consistently conducting "After Action Reviews" is a popular practice that promotes reflection. Some companies support "focus Fridays" or other segments of the week when meetings are discouraged and employees have time to think. Embedding these types of systems into company routines signals to employees that *leadership values the learning* that comes from their reflection on the work. *Investing in processes and systems* that set expectations for sharing of the lessons learned completes the cycle of behavior that represents a learning organization.

What does it mean for a learning executive (senior-most executive responsible for learning and development) role to be meaningfully integrated with the CEO and the Board?

The pace of change in business has made learning a competitive imperative for all levels of employees in any corporation. The learning executive should be fully integrated into the CEO and the Board's considerations of the company's talent. Any review of strategy, short-term or longer term, includes a discussion of the best talent to put toward strategic efforts to achieve the best results. At this stage, there should be an evaluation of this talent and any opportunities for development identified for the learning leader to address. Proactively planning learning that can be built into business processes, rather than waiting for a gap to appear as a mistake, a miss, or a delay, is the real, new, and important role for the learning executive.

How can a learning executive develop and deepen a foundation of trust within a company in order to facilitate strategy and learning integration initiatives?

The learning executive must be placed in the organization . . . or at least viewed . . . as a business enabler. The first shift is to frame learning as a business activity. Many leaders value management and leadership learning but consider this classic "HR activity" as outside of the business core. To convince business leaders that learning is a critical part of the strategy discussion, the learning executive must be versed and credible in business strategy and business measures and deliver solutions that support strategic outcomes.

I like the way that P&G talks about strategy, using the Monitor Group's method of cascading choices for competitive strategy. With this framework, the business decides where it will play and how it will win . . . and then defines the organizational capabilities that are required and the management structures necessary to support them. This is the perfect insertion point for the learning leader to propose learning initiatives that are clearly aligned to the strategy.

A discussion about capabilities includes identification of both the behaviors and the knowledge and skills required to hit the target. Language is important and talking in terms of "building capabilities" as opposed to "providing training" puts the learning leader in a more impactful position. A strong learning leader will integrate multiple talent management strategies in proposed solutions (such as job assignments or executive coaching, in addition to training programs). Trust, then, is built through sustained success in contributing to the achievement of the strategic goals.

How can a learning executive maximize coordination with stakeholders, both internal and external?

The learning executive operates at an executive level and, as such, is responsible for relationships within the organization as well as outside of it. This work occupies much more of the learning executive's time than the actual development or delivery of learning solutions.

Internally, the learning leader must understand how the business works and how each business unit or function contributes to the success of the organization. This is the frame each internal stakeholder will bring to needs discussions. Additionally, because learning executives work horizontally across the organization, they have opportunities to see connections and synergies, as well as common gaps in skills and capabilities. A cross-functional view and the respect of multiple functions allows the learning executive to suggest collaboration between internal groups that can look like efficiency, innovation, or some other business enablement.

Externally, the learning executive needs a keen grip on market conditions and customer needs to build the capabilities in employees and managers that deliver the company's brand promise. The learning leader is also responsible for staying in touch with thought leaders on the business of learning at work. Changes in the learning industry happen as rapidly as for other areas of businesses. (Balancing true connection between future-focused needs of the organization and upcoming trends in L&D can be tricky, as vendors often position their products in ways that look like innovation.) A strong learning executive will make connections with others in similar roles and look objectively at the products and practices of like companies along with disruptive methods occurring in diverse industries or academia, so the organization's capabilities stay relevant.

If the learning function is responsible for learning in the "extended enterprise," along with employee development, then customers and suppliers to the business become stakeholders and providing learning to these partners is an additional business enabler.

How can the learning executive distill knowledge both up and down the information chain of the company?

The knowledge and skills developed in the day-to-day experience of work create by far the most significant amount of learning needed to distill and share within an organization. To acknowledge and capture this tacit information, the learning executive needs to promote two important concepts as part of the organizational culture. The first is a 70:20:10 development philosophy and the second is a Leaders as Teachers component in leadership programming. These work together to put more emphasis on practical, actionable, and immediate *learning from others,* as opposed to the more traditional theory and academic-style learning from expert sessions. When learning leaders recall their remit as improving business performance, these strategies become critical levers to extract and distribute knowledge both up and down in the organization.

Several years ago, the Center for Creative Leadership conducted a series of studies to understand how employees learn from their work experiences. The questions explored: "What experiences have the most developmental impact?" and "Who will benefit the most from such experiences?" The analysis and results are summarized in the book titled *The Lessons of Experience* by McCall, Lombardo, and Morrison. It was discovered that approximately 70 percent of what people need to know to do their jobs, they learn from job experiences, 20 percent from relationships with other people, and only a small portion (10 percent) from traditional training and materials. In this era of rapid change, many large corporations are embracing this logic for a number of reasons. Nigel Paine, in his book *The Learning Challenge*, cites several compelling reasons why learning leaders need to find new ways of thinking about learning at work, like this 70:20:10 model, including the fact that courses on their own will not create a learning organization or empower staff to take control of their own learning. The dotting of courses throughout the calendar year tends to isolate learning from work—separating the need to share knowledge from the learning process.

The Leaders as Teachers approach is practiced by many companies also. For a practical guide to implementing in leadership learning programs, look for books by Edward T. Betof. What I see at P&G goes beyond a Leaders as Teachers program organized by the learning leader. As part of the company's DNA and its 177-year history, there is a commitment by all leaders to coach, teach and mentor others. It is a management accountability to develop the capability of their team, as individuals and as a performing unit. This is one of the reasons that P&G is so often at the top of lists ranking companies best at developing leaders. As Noel Tichy wrote in *The Leadership Engine* that winning companies have transcended from being *learning* organizations to *teaching* organizations—both have the goal of ensuring the transfer of knowledge and skills, but the latter also prioritizing that individuals pass on their learning to others.

Once incubated, how can companies institutionalize the inclusion of learning plans in corporate strategies?

To institutionalize the inclusion of learning plans in corporate strategies, I'm a fan of Robert Brinkerhoff's Learning Impact Maps. The Impact Map is simple and avoids the "needs assessment" trap of creating a laundry list of classroom training interventions for the business. It also allows the learning leader to talk to business leaders in business language instead of "learning-speak." The Impact Map has four categories and works backwards from organizational goals. When complete then, a well-designed Impact Map will detail (1) the knowledge and skills an employee needs, (2) the behaviors or actions that will be driven be the new knowledge and skills, (3) the results the business should realize because of the new behaviors, and (4) how these results will help accomplish the organizational goals. The true shift that learning leaders must make to function successfully in this space is to realize that their job is not about individual learning and development but about improving performance for the organization.

How can companies ensure that recommendations for initiatives are data driven?

Many companies call on their learning executives for "training issues" and their resolution. Learning leaders must take a leadership role in making sure initiatives are data driven by first ensuring the needs are data driven. Historically hungry to demonstrate proficiency in delivery training or simply happy to be asked to engage with the business, many L&D departments have accepted a senior leader's assertion that "we need training" without engaging in a consulting conversation that verifies a training need exists. This is a very short-sighted approach, because providing training, when a lack of skills or knowledge is not the root reason for poor performance, dooms the solution. Performance will not improve and resources spent on a training solution will be wasted. The credibility of the learning function will suffer subsequently.

Most learning leaders are guilty of "making balloon animals" or providing some other sort of "edutainment" at the request of a senior leader. These requests sound something like this: *"I'm bringing my whole team in next week for three days. I want to include some development for them. What can you do that's fun and will build good feelings in the team? I can give you 45 minutes."* As long as the learning executive and the L&D function are willing to fulfill these requests rather than push for true development needs and the allocation of time and resources to build actual capability, they will continue to play on the sidelines of the business.

How can companies ensure that measurement and reassessment of strategy/learning initiatives are ongoing?

An industry-led initiative called "Talent Development Reporting Principles" will help standardize and define consistent measures for employee development which can enable firms in consistent and ongoing measurement and assessment of learning strategies and initiatives.

In 2010, Kent Barnett from Knowledge Advisors and Tamar Elkeles of Qualcomm launched a groundbreaking effort to bring standard principles and reporting to all human capital processes. Together they led a group of learning and measurement thought leaders and prominent practitioners, in the development of guiding principles, standard measures, statements and reports, much like the "Generally Accepted Accounting Principles" (GAAP) provided for accountants.

The statements are intended to organize and standardize all the important L&D measures just as an income statement, balance sheet and cash flow statement measure business activity.

For learning initiatives this group recommends three executive reports be used to manage the learning function and to deliver planned results. An L&D

Summary Report is the highest level report and is to be used with the CEO and other senior leaders. The other two are the L&D Program Report and the L&D Operations Report, intended to be used by the learning executive to manage program effectiveness and overall efficiency.

Leading learning executives are looking at ways of adopting this industry-led recommendation to shift and scale learning metrics up from activity measures that doesn't provide much relevance to the business scorecard. Percentage of seats filled makes little difference if knowledge and skills are not transferred back to the workplace representing increased capability and stronger results.

Another new development that will have broad-reaching impact on learning measurement is the introduction of a brand new learning technology specification called the "Tin Can API." Tracking completion of an instructor-led workshop or an e-learning course have been the best measures available to date on how employees are learning. Yet, learning leaders know that much learning happens outside of these two modes of delivery . . . such as through conversations, accessing online materials, or sessions with experts, coaches, or mentors. Tracking these sorts of "informal" learning has eluded learning leaders until now. The Tin Can API (also known as Experience API or "xAPI") tracks "experiences" learners have—rather than course completion. Now learning leaders can track completing a course as well as activities like playing games, reading a blog or viewing a video. Learning executives are starting to ask their learning management providers (LMS) and other systems for Tin Can compliance.

Index

About the Author

Jason Wingard is Managing Director and Chief Learning Officer at Goldman Sachs, a global investment banking, securities, and investment management firm. In this role, he is responsible for the strategy and implementation of learning and leadership development solutions for the firm's global workforce and select clients. He is also President and CEO of The Education Board, Inc., a management consulting firm specializing in organizational strategy, executive coaching, and facilitation.

Previously, Jason served as Vice Dean of Executive Education and Adjunct Professor of Management at the Wharton School of the University of Pennsylvania. At Wharton, he led one of the world's largest providers of leadership development programs and advisory services for managers and executives. Prior to Wharton, Jason held a variety of cross-functional executive and consulting roles at ePals, Inc., Stanford University, the Aspen Institute, the Vanguard Group, and Silicon Graphics.

During his career, Jason has gained experience and provided customized leadership and professional development solutions for a variety of sectors including corporate, not-for-profit, sports and entertainment, higher